MORE PROFIT, LESS RISK

Other books by Charles A. Cerami:

ALLIANCE BORN OF DANGER
CRISIS: THE LOSS OF EUROPE

MORE PROFIT, LESS RISK: YOUR NEW FINANCIAL STRATEGY

by
Charles A. Cerami

McGRAW-HILL BOOK COMPANY

New York   St. Louis   San Francisco
Toronto   Mexico   Sydney

1 2 3 4 5 6 7 8 9 D O D O 8 7 6 5 4 3 2

ISBN 0-07-010324-0

LIBRARY OF CONGRESS CATALOGING IN PUBLICATION DATA

Cerami, Charles A.
More profit, less risk: your new financial strategy.
1. Finance, Personal. 2. Investments. I. Title.
HG179.C47   332.024   82-7775
ISBN 0-07-010324-0   AACR2

Book design by Stan Drate.

Contents

INTRODUCTION   *xi*

PART I
THE TWO ECONOMIC PHASES AHEAD

1 WHERE POLITICS AND POLICIES ARE
   TAKING US   *3*

   Quick pick-up, then worsening inflation / Three
   myths / Cuts in federal income taxes will
   continue / Federal deficits will balloon, then
   recede / A major jump in foreign aid / Profits up,
   stocks way up / Inflation and interest rates will push
   higher / The U.S. dollar will tumble in value around
   the world / Soaring gold and silver / The rewards for
   investors

2 A PERIOD OF RECOVERY IS AHEAD   *14*

   Why stocks reverse their course / And how bonds
   will contribute / Why most forecasts will prove
   wrong / Enormous change on the way / The dark
   side of progress / New paths for old investments

3 Your Twin Goals: More Profit,
Less Risk   23

First, your balance sheet / Two true stories / Second,
the key questions / New view of your prospects /
The three criteria: multiplying power, stability,
flexibility

4 Why You Must Diversify   32

Dividing your capital / Averaging is better than
timing / Dividing your hedges / Balancing your
stocks / Safeguarding your capital

5 Investing versus Speculating   41

Knowing the difference / Weighing risk and reward in
stocks, bonds, utilities, real estate, diamonds,
commodities, stock options, antiques and
collectibles / The importance of fashion / Dividing
your two roles

PART II

QUICK PROFIT-BUILDING
STRATEGIES

6 Watching the Arabs
for Profit Clues   55

Lessons the Arabs learned / Gold from $250 to
$800 / Where OPEC money is now / The advice they
are getting / Long-term loans and bonds / Reading
what money managers read

7 What You Should Know about
the Stock Market   65

The best barometer / Why the market
knows / Which average to follow / A simple

approach / What to watch for / The question of
time / Reacting to signals / Charts: "A picture of
what people are doing"

8   QUICK IN-AND-OUT TRADING OF STOCKS   77

Power of the unknown / Signal to sell / Moves to
watch for / The market versus the news / How cash
fuels stocks / The money supply / Three vital
signs / Betting against first reactions

9   BUYING SHARES IN COMPANIES   87

Where to study / Spotting winners early / The
general climate / The growing industries / Selecting
companies / Low price, high gain

10   WHAT BONDS AND SAVINGS
     CAN DO FOR YOU   97

A key figure / The basic moves / Your personal
situation / "High-yield" bonds / Tax-free
bonds / Compounding power

11   MONEY MARKET FUNDS:
     TOO GOOD TO BE TRUE?   108

Start of a new idea / Choosing your money market
fund / When to put money in / When to move money
out / Your overall cash management

PART III

ENSURING LONG-TERM
SECURITY

12   GOLD—THE MISUNDERSTOOD METAL   119

The ideal money / The measuring rod / The
underlying reason / Gold's uses to you

13   WHY YOU SHOULD OWN GOLD COINS   *128*

1933 and now / Coins are best / Rare and
not-so-rare / At any time of life / Five "best"
coins / Where to buy / Keeping gold safe / For the
bold or the wary

14   GOLD-MINE STOCKS—FOR INCOME
AND APPRECIATION   *139*

Buy mines, not holding companies / South African
and other mines / Driefontein—a super-mine / Vaal
Reefs—another leader / Kloof—a special
advantage / Short-life mines / Gold plus uranium

15   THE SILVER ROLLER COASTER   *147*

The historical price ratio / The great move / Three
points to remember / When, how, and why to buy
silver coins, bars, options, futures

PART IV

UNUSUAL WAYS TO MAKE YOUR MONEY GROW

16   OPTIONS—SAFE WAYS TO BUY
AND SELL   *159*

What is an option? / The selling side / A fully
insured method

17   TRADING COMMODITIES—
EVEN FOR CONSERVATIVES   *166*

What is leverage? / Conservative trading / Futures
contracts as insurance / With help or on your
own? / The whipsaw problem / Smoothing the

action / Numbers win over hunches / Holding on to
your gains / The names of the game

18 TRADING MONEY TO MAKE MONEY   *180*

Trading two foreign currencies / The preferred
method / What affects a currency? / Keeping
posted / Trading currencies for the cautious
businessman

19 GETTING INCOME FROM YOUR GOLD
    AND SILVER   *189*

When not to start / A steady income booster / Using
the gold-silver relationship / Special use of mining
stocks / A special way to trade commodities
risk-free / Two precautions

20 THE NEXT GREAT STARS—
    THE MORE-THAN-PRECIOUS MINERALS   *200*

Risk of a cut-off / Worsening trend / The potential
for gains / Buying Australian mining stocks / Buying
minerals / The steps in trading / Some
recommended metals

21 PUTTING ALL THIS TOGETHER
    TO FORM YOUR FINANCIAL STRATEGY   *209*

The different stages in your career / Sample plans to
choose from / Remember the safety net / Doing it
your way.

INDEX   *217*

Introduction

Everyone needs a financial adviser. Even a business expert needs one, just as an intelligent lawyer wants another counsel to handle his case. Among other reasons, it is essential to have an outside person look objectively at your affairs and see them without emotion. And apart from that, even the most knowledgeable person can overlook obvious opportunities and pitfalls.

This book is, as nearly as I can make it, your personal financial planner. Just as if you came to me for advice on your investments, I will tell you some very simple things you can do to make safe profits, a number of methods that are more complex, and a few highly sophisticated techniques. I will also explain the pros and cons of each one and steer you toward those that I feel are best suited to your situation. And I will give my reasoning for each piece of advice because that's what I would do if you came to see me in person. I think you should know the facts behind any financial strategy even if it takes a little more time to absorb.

This will be done against my background in national and international economics. Both are essential in forming a plan that will stand up to the changes and crises that we face. I know that in planning for your future, you are caught between the gloomy prophets of economic doom and the chronic optimists who insist that America will somehow come out on top because she always has before. Hearing the two, you are left to wonder: Should I risk putting my money into stocks that may evaporate? Or should I invest it mainly in gold and other "hard" assets that may go into a dormant state for years to come?

So we will look together at the one key question, which is really at the heart of everybody's personal planning: *whether to bet on growth or disaster*. I will give you my own answer and my reasons for believing that an early opportunity to make money with dynamic investments is shaping up. This will be followed by a new economics crisis. I will tell you how to keep your profits safe in that second and longer phase.

You do not have to agree with my outlook in order to find that the approaches I suggest will be useful to you. I do not believe in strategies that are based solely on a single long-range projection, because it is like flying a plane with just enough fuel to suit the meteorologist's present forecast. Most of the chapters in this book will prepare you for different kinds of economic weather and not just for the one that I consider most likely.

What you need is not just a set of facts. Most people, including some very knowledgeable ones, make the same mistakes that have historically trapped investors: They put too many eggs in *one* basket. And they always pick the same basket that everyone else is using at that time. Inevitably a lot of eggs get broken.

This book should give you enough varied investment techniques to allow you to have your assets in several "baskets" at any one time, even if your total wealth is small for the moment. It will deal with your own situation—whether you are a young investor whose free capital is very limited or a retiree who has to move more cautiously than he used to do when there was a steady inflow of new money every month. Whatever your position, I will show you how to combine two or more techniques into an overall financial program that fits your present needs and your hopes for the future. And I will make many suggestions about timing that can keep you moving ahead of the crowd.

Just one more word before we start in earnest to understand the state of our economy and to talk over together what you should be doing about it: Waste no time regretting what you failed to do earlier. When the professionals who make not only a living, but also a fortune, on Wall Street lock their desks at night they often say: "Well, the markets will be open again tomorrow." They will be for you too.

Charles A. Cerami

I

THE TWO ECONOMIC PHASES AHEAD

1

Where Politics and Policies Are Taking Us

I see a new kind of economic pattern shaping up for the rest of the 1980's. It will be a fast two-step movement: First, an upturn. Then, in two to three years, a renewal of serious inflation, soaring interest rates, and loss of investor confidence.

Inflation is being dampened temporarily by methods that cannot be continued. Not only our government, but most governments in the free world, are edging toward the idea that UNEMPLOYMENT is a more immediate problem than rising prices. With differing words and actions, they will all start giving top priority to *fighting joblessness rather than inflation.*

This will stimulate business and create the illusion of returning prosperity. It will offer tremendous opportunities to invest, profit, and get ready for the longer run. I will tell you how to use that time to make solid gains and arrange for more security in the turbulent years to follow.

It is important to understand, first of all, what the present political leaders are trying to do and how much of it is realistic. Having inherited the most complex economic crisis in our history, the Republican Administration and its friends in the Congress and Senate are trying to keep intact the small remaining kernel of the conservative revolution they headed after the last presidential election. They have made a historic effort, but most of their stated goals—to balance the budget, sharply reduce the size of government, swiftly enlarge our

3

armed might, and bring efficient management to replace a chaotic economy—have had to be shelved or "stretched out" to some future time. What looked like genuinely different approaches at the start of 1981 have had to be diluted until most of them are hard to distinguish from what the Democrats would be doing in the same circumstances.

Three Myths

The Reagan team, by oversimplifying the problems it inherited, went seriously astray on three subjects that forced the problem to be turned inside out:

- The promise to move quickly toward balancing the budget was ill-judged. It should have been stated as a very long-term goal, not an early one. The myth that 30 or 50 billion dollars makes all the difference between success or failure in managing an economy of 3 trillion dollars has been very destructive. This almost irrelevant point became a shackle that hampered the much more important steps to rebuild investment and productivity. It prevented the even larger tax cuts that could have made a profound difference and, instead, it substituted a creeping approach that falls short on most counts.
- The problem of future inflation was greatly increased by going along for so many months with the Federal Reserve Board notion that forcing interest rates higher was a way to fight the inflationary ills. What Chairman John Volcker did was to inject a huge new cost factor—the higher cost of money—into the economy. This again was substituting a short-term goal for a longer and more solid one. For while appearing to diminish inflation for a time, it fueled the much greater flames that are going to burst around us by 1985.
- And the program made no serious attempt to do the one thing that has always been needed to really cure financial troubles: To ask everyone to tighten belts and live a little poorer for a time. Imposing austerity on a relatively few

welfare recipients accomplishes little. It is the far greater number of employed persons—the bulk of the population—that determines success or failure. When a family, a company, or a nation runs on hard times, an essential ingredient of the cure is to ask everyone to make do with a little less. If politics makes it impossible for a government to impose that on both labor and management, the end result is not hard to foresee. Washington has not dared to go beyond suggesting some limitation on the amount of wage *increases*. But any increase of buying power means that even more money will be out in the marketplace bidding prices higher.

Many people from all over the country who phone me to talk about their investments grasp this faster than some of the officials do. A Kansas farmer recently told me, "I think Reaganomics started out without realizing that a sick economy needs something different from a healthy one." Principles that were once "sound" when our economy was sleek and efficient were assumed to be equally right for curing its ills. But a training program for athletes is not appropriate to the sick room. A monetary policy that would have preserved stability several decades ago is totally unsuitable when a bloated money supply needs to be *slashed* rather than stabilized. And an interest-rate policy that penalizes indebtedness is disastrous when the government itself is mired in debt, *has* to keep borrowing more, and is, therefore, the principal victim of the high rates.

1. Cuts in Federal Income Taxes Will Continue

Reducing all these trends to practical politics, I know from inside sources that President Reagan is faced with a choice between abandoning either his tax policies or his fight on inflation. A terrible dilemma. But despite a temporary pullback, he will keep most of the fundamental tax changes and let inflation win another round. For the tax law—the 1981 Economic Recovery Act—is that "remaining kernel" of the Reagan program that has not been discarded.

President Reagan's reasoning, I think, will be that the shape of taxes can start the permanent return to healthy levels of investment and productivity, while inflation, destructive as it is, might be fought more effectively a little later. To understand this, you must bear in mind that taxes are not just one segment of a country's bookkeeping; they are the key numbers that determine what kind of society it will be. Who keeps how much of what he earns, who can or cannot amass substantial wealth, and whether people can actually aspire to move up to a higher economic level—these facts can remake a nation. Without ever putting it in those terms, the Reagan team believes that such incentives can make a vital and prosperous country, while the lack of them produces an equality that ultimately makes life equally bad for all. That is why the White House will insist on letting the third tax cut take effect in mid-1983 despite so many short-term objections to it.

Can this policy prevent a severe loss of Reagan prestige in the last half of his term? Quite possibly. The record has not been good enough to avoid a decline in the Republican standing in Congress; but tax cuts and the approaching end of a recession can be sold to the people as evidence that the program deserves more chance to develop.

2. Federal Deficits Will Balloon, Then Recede

The 1984 elections will depend on the delicate timing of business conditions. The recovery in 1983 and 1984 will favor the G.O.P. And the federal deficits that are now soaring will start to come down as this prosperity boosts tax revenues—another plus for the Republicans. But by November, 1984, the U.S. economy will be on the verge of years when high inflation and a new round of interest-rate pressures will hit hard.

A resurgent Democratic Party will be able to make all the charges and all the seductive promises that are always open to the opposition. Just as candidate Franklin D. Roosevelt once attacked President Herbert Hoover for running a budget deficit, the Democrats of 1984 will maintain they are so full of fiscal responsibility that they deplore the Reagan deficit. "We can balance the budget by expansive measures—spurring the pace of business and increasing tax revenues without higher rates," they will point out. But foreseeing that, the White House will already be saying much the same thing. If the present Federal Reserve Board chairman gets in the way with tight-money policies, the next appointee will be chosen in 1983 to avoid that roadblock. And the word to the nation's voters will be: "Now that we have government spending down and the tax laws are more equitable, Phase I is completed, and it's time to put some new speed into the American machine."

If this seems to have only faint resemblance to the "conservative revolution" that some expected from the landslide of 1980, remember neither that election nor any other produced any victory for the principle of belt-tightening or economic austerity. The promise was to cut spending with only minimum pain—and especially to cut taxes. So there is no reason to believe that the voters will insist on austerity in the next election or the one after that.

3. A Major Jump in Foreign Aid

Astonishingly, I am convinced that an America fighting against record deficits and the weakness of its own currency is going to swing back to a form of spending that is usually associated with days of great affluence. The Republican incumbent will soon be explaining that a large new program of credits to the developing nations must be started.

But this will have nothing to do with the despised idea of "giveaway plans." Although a few words of altruism will be injected, total self-interest will be the foundation this time. Every one of my talks with foreign policy officials reflects this.

The simple fact is that American business urgently needs new markets. Not just here at home, for so many of our wants are already satisfied. But overseas as well, in lands that are hungry for almost every sort of product and service. And even more than America, the Europeans and the Japanese need outlets for their goods in order to keep from being crushed by unemployment. It is another form of self-interest for us to be certain that allied countries do not tumble into chaos or into the hands of unfriendly regimes. So both for ourselves and for our alliances, we will take part in an enlarged program of world development. Some of this will be done by contributing more to the World Bank and other international lending agencies. But much of it will be in the form of direct loans from the United States to the poorer nations. They will be what are called "tied loans"—meaning that the money will be spent only to buy goods or services from America. And many forms of special help will be proposed for American companies that take their skills abroad to develop the Third World.

Some of this will be like reinventing old principles. But after twenty years of steadily deriding and shrinking such programs, the ideas will seem fairly fresh. And this time they will even get some support from organized labor, which can have a strong effect on the Congress, because their potential for creating export sales and *jobs at home* will be stressed.

4. Profits Up, Stocks Way Up

How, you will ask, can this clearly inflationary policy point to anything but worse troubles? How can we find opportunity in any of this?

First, there is some truth in what the Reagan supporters will be claiming. They *have* made some corrections that will give American business a little more traction to get moving. And as I said earlier, even the frightening federal deficit will start to subside in 1984 because of this business upturn. The effect on our stock market will be spectacular.

The above-mentioned 1981 Economic Recovery Act actually redefines the role of government in this country, *reversing* Franklin D. Roosevelt's moves of the early 1930's. Before this law, Washington had been expected to take almost 23% of the economy's total earnings by 1984; now it will tax away just over 19%. This difference of about $140 billion annually will stay in private hands instead of being handled by government. This assumes that government spending and borrowing will also be restrained. The legislators will be under pressure to keep up such restraint because some of the Act's fine print says that after 1985 the Congress cannot increase spending faster than the rate of economic growth, unless it also votes for higher taxes, which would be politically unpalatable.

Even more important, there will be many incentives for private businesses to invest more and for individuals to save more. Faster depreciation on buildings, machinery, and vehicles will create more purchases of these items and will also leave more profits in corporate hands—to be used for growth or for dividends. Either way, they will make it more attractive to be a stockholder. So will the cut in the maximum tax on capital gains.

The coming new injection of stimulants into the economy, which would have been deadly two years ago, can now give it another period of pseudo-prosperity. And the sheer size of the American juggernaut gives it a great momentum of its own, apart from the rights or wrongs of government. Having just struggled, like a massive trailer truck, up one hard hill, it is now set to roll on down the other side regardless of how well its engine is actually running. For example, I foresee the following surges:

- The housing industry will come back to life. The pent-up demand for new housing will create fine sales.
- And new home buyers will have a great hunger for carpeting, furniture, appliances, garden equipment—all the "big ticket" items that spur other retail sales.
- The auto industry, aided by the technological breakthroughs on fuel consumption, will also benefit greatly from the stimulus.
- And a post-recession feeling that it is time to buy and travel and enjoy again will brighten the atmosphere.

The underlying problems of a newly deteriorating dollar and a relapse into double-digit inflation will prevent outright euphoria, but it will not stop the wheels from turning. There

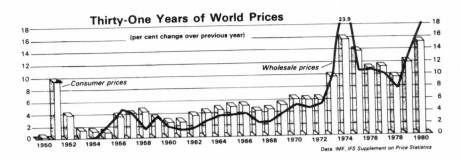

Thirty-One Years of World Prices

(per cent change over previous year)

is something of an "après nous, le déluge" spirit in all this, but having delayed the day of reckoning so long, "who knows whether we might not put it off a lot longer," as one government official recently told me hopefully.

5. Inflation and Interest Rates Will Push Higher

That way of dealing with debts always makes them mount. The new round of inflation will carry us to higher figures than the last. Interest rates will also tend to move upward again. But as it is realized that high interest rates will not be a cure and that they are actually adding to inflation in two ways, there will be open talk of deferring or canceling the interest portion of America's public debt. Since any such failure to meet federal obligations would be a form of bankruptcy, officials will deny it as strongly as they once denied that the dollar would ever be devalued. Faced with a new crisis, they will probably swing back to an easy-money policy—pretending to believe that a new wave of expansion would fight inflation by increasing productivity and tax revenues. In reality, it will just be a way to buy more time.

6. The U.S. Dollar Will Tumble in Value Around the World

There is more money than ever in the U.S. economy and more dollars floating all over the world. And this cash is not coun-

terbalanced by more American merchandise or more productivity. The classic recipe for global inflation—and depreciation of the world's chief currency—keeps being used on a
larger scale.

The temporary strength of the American dollar in the early
1980's will soon be seen to have been a mirage. Its condition
will worsen markedly, creating anxiety in 1983 and 1984. Because domestic business will be strong in those years, the
United States will import heavily. *Imports will far exceed
exports*—and that will increase both inflation and unemployment. The U.S. trade deficit with Japan, in particular, will
again rise dramatically. In all my travels, I see evidences that
protectionist forces to curb imports will put greater pressure
on many congressmen and at least a third of the senators
(those who are up for reelection), threatening one of every six
manufacturing jobs here that depend on foreign trade. And
sales to developing countries, which have become vital markets for the United States and Europe, will weaken because
our mindless interest-rate policy of 1981–82 heaped such
massive finance costs on those nations that they had to cut
their growth.

You will see more and more headlines about new currency
crises and a run on the dollar overseas, as in the 1970's. Since
this will come at a time when most foreign currencies are
more suspect than they were in the earlier decade, the rush to
get rid of most paper money will be even more hectic than
before.

But I assure you that the U.S. dollar will not collapse entirely or be replaced by a new currency in a different color, as
some grim forecasters often predict. They overlook the interesting seesaw that provides a basic safeguard: As inflation
erodes the dollar's buying power and sends the price of gold
higher, the gold owned by the U.S. government increases in
value too. This gain gives the *falling* dollar an ever-*rising*
gold backing. And that will be enough to prevent complete
loss of confidence in U.S. money. But since foreign governments are no longer allowed to exchange dollars for U.S. gold,
there is nothing to prevent a sharp fall in its value abroad.

7. Soaring Gold and Silver

When people, institutions, and nations try to get out of paper money, they exchange it for tangible assets. This puts upward pressure on the prices of all such articles. So collectibles, antiques, fine rugs, art objects, and gemstones will again rise in price, although I am lukewarm about even the best of them as investments because I doubt that they will entirely recover from the sharp losses they took in 1981. *Gold and silver, on the other hand, will go far beyond their old highs.* The difference is that some of those other tangibles were promoted and merchandised as being absolutely safe against declines. The fact that the DeBeers cartel controls diamond sales, for example, had been used to "prove" that diamonds could never fall far. But DeBeers lost control of the market for a time, and most investors have relearned the old European maxim: "The easiest thing in the world is to buy a diamond; the hardest thing in the world is to sell it."

But precious metals were known all along to be potentially volatile, to move in concert with prevailing economic forces and, most important of all, to be completely and perfectly "liquid." They can always be sold instantly and for the full market price. To say that gold will rise in price, just after I have said that the dollar will fall, is not just a matter of opinion. It is actually a matter of simple arithmetic. The gold price is set in dollars—even in the London and Zurich markets where most of it is traded. So the equation works exactly like the two sides of an old-fashioned scale. When one goes down, the other must go up, and vice versa.

If the dollar's average value in all the different foreign exchange markets of the world goes down by 10%, then it will take about 10% more dollars to buy any tangible item that is traded on a worldwide basis. So, allowing for the various monetary deviations that happen in such a widespread network of buyers and sellers, gold will also command a dollar price about 10% higher just on that basis alone. Now gold may go up a lot more than that for other reasons; it usually does. For the mere fact that the dollar is seen to be falling frightens many investors into thinking that other adverse happenings are on the way; and they buy more gold. Since there is so little of this metal, any such demand for it usually sends the price up more swiftly and sharply than would be the case with a more abundant commodity.

I foresee that gold will exceed *$1,000 per ounce during 1983*. Based on typical market behavior, it is then likely to drop back considerably, because a great many investors who are waiting for this event will believe that it is time to sell. But the world's economic situation will not permit the price to stay down as long as it normally would. It will move back up and very substantially beyond the $1,000 level.

Silver—plus platinum, palladium, rhodium, osmium, and several other of the lesser precious metals—will move right along with gold. There will be variations in the speed of movement. But each of these has a normal relationship to the gold price and will roughly parallel it. In the case of silver, this points to a price that will at least slightly exceed the old $50 high. I believe the supply-demand picture indicates it will go much further than that, but it may take several more years.

The net effect of happenings outlined above will give a powerful boost to the rewards that you as an investor can expect. Regrettably, we will not enjoy the happy sort of boom that comes after a long depressed period. Starting from a point when years of prosperity and inflation had left our plants loaded with more machinery than they can use, the people loaded with more goods than they need, and the banking institutions loaded with more money than we should ever have had, this will be an uneven resurgence.

That's the world opening up ahead of us. Keep in mind how both the early trends and the subsequent ones predicted in this chapter can be used as a basis for many specific profit-making techniques.

2

A Period of Recovery Is Ahead

I firmly believe the most hectic financial years of this century are immediately ahead of us. More people will be getting rich in the next few years; far more will be getting hurt in the years that follow. It will no longer be possible just to get along fairly well financially. There will be some big winners, many big losers, and few in between.

Many new companies, products, and methods will shoot to the fore. I will indicate how you—whether you are a new investor or a retiree—can bet on the right ones and thrive along with them, even though the foundations of their success will be unsteady. Unsteady because the money we use is questionable, the values of our belongings are overstated, the conditions of our banks and savings institutions are unsound.

No one can give really firm and rational arguments for great confidence in long-term stability. It seems very nearly certain that a crash will be necessary in order to bring relative values back to normal and permit new foundations to be established. But not just yet. That crash will not be "needed" for some years to come because we already had one of the great crashes of recent history—the stock and bond markets from 1974 to 1981 were reduced to bedrock levels. So a period of recovery from the 1970's will be ahead of us.

Why Stocks Reverse Their Course

"Why does a long decline in stock and bond prices lay any sort of foundation for a lengthy upward move?" This very question was put to me in an investment meeting, and it is a normal one. The reason is this: A long-depressed stock market means that virtually all of American industry has been held too cheap.

An oversight of this sort by investors around the world is the type of major financial error that occurs only a few times in a century. Imagine what it really signifies: that the millions of potential stock buyers in the United States and abroad looked at the whole of America's economy and thought it worth only a third or a fourth of what its value would normally have been in this period. If they were all correct, then the stock collapse would have been signaling and anticipating an industrial crash of unprecedented proportions. If wrong, as I believe, the amount of stock buying, the number of transactions, the readjustment of values required for all these people to correct their holdings is mind-boggling.

Naturally this would be accompanied by a creation of huge, new wealth, for bear in mind that as stocks go up, new buying power is created without taking away from anyone. Each person who profitably passes along a share of stock to another buyer at a higher price has cash that never existed before put into his account. And the investor who holds stock that is valued at a higher price can borrow on it and create for himself a source of growing purchasing power from one day to the next.

And How Bonds Will Contribute

Similarly, you must realize why a bond market that stays unusually low signifies that investors may have formed another kind of misjudgment. This time it is about the true future value of the U.S. dollar. While the bond market's gloomy forebodings are less apt to be wrong than those of the stock market, the likelihood of even intermediate rallies from such a low condition implies creation of another form of new wealth. The two markets—stocks and bonds—taken together can suddenly add so much more usable buying power to our economy that they provide the same sort of boomy potential as would be the case in a post-war period when many industries are on the point of surging ahead and creating more jobs.

To imagine that these markets might go far down, instead of up, is very difficult. Some slippage is always possible, but obviously small compared to the potential gains. That is why such a reversal of trend usually goes on for rather a long time. The fear that one incident or another might nip it in the bud should carry little weight. Sudden accidents seldom make a great difference in the cycles of financial history; economic and political trends develop over long periods of time. They are like tidal waves that can wash right over the apparent importance of a revolt here or an assassination there. A dead president, or sheik, might cause a world war only if the war was looking for an excuse to happen and the troops were already in place. The underlying forces of today are a reaction not only against the decline of the 1970's but also against many excesses of the preceding five decades. The pendulum that took so long to swing in one direction will move the other way until the mid-1980's.

Why Most Forecasts Will Prove Wrong

Narrowing the focus from the broad economy to some specific lines of business that make it up, I would disagree with the many analysts who think our industries are going into a steadily retreating phase. It is popular to say that higher energy costs have ended our years of expansion and turned us toward a long new era of gradual contraction.

These other analysts see that our economic pace has already slackened. And they feel that the inflation, the growth, the energy revolution of the last decade have set up a situation in which a progressive slowing down of all these things must come. A shrinking of activity; a gradually slowing pace to cure the excessive speed of the past.

That is not only wrong. It cannot *possibly* be right. In a world of uncertainty one economic fact *is* sure: Forecasts based on smooth adjustments of a very volatile movement will always be wrong. A slow period may be followed by another quiet one. But a wild period will always bring on a series of strong fluctuations before the forces are exhausted. Some future prospects are a matter of opinion and could go either way; but this one is a matter of arithmetic plus human nature and cannot conceivably go the way most observers are predicting.

The inflation has been far too great for too long. The amount of excess money floating around the country and the world could not be "soaked up" and returned to sound finance without several decades of consistently tightened belts on the part of almost everyone. Talking with many persons of all ages and conditions each week, I am convinced that people just won't be compliant enough to exist that way. The very young who had no part in making or enjoying the inflation will not tamely live the bulk of their lives in scrimping mediocrity and pay out huge sums in social security and other transfers to the elders who put them into that bind. So a long, slow pay-off of the debts that began before midcentury is virtually out of the question. Instead, the political leaders will be forced to arrange a burst of fresh activity to drown the old debts in a sea of new money, which will eventually lead to a big smash. People will then be forced to scrimp and be grateful for the barest existence. If they are *forced*, then it is possible; but accept it and live peaceably with it they will not.

Enormous Change on the Way

This view of the future is, as I said, based on an analysis of what is happening now, in the present. We have lost our way, but not our vitality. I know for a fact that the drawing boards of America are full of new developments that will add up to enormous change—away from what has happened since the 1930's. Change in governmental ways, for one thing. It is clear that government spending is not really going to be cut as much as the original Reagan team insisted and that the U.S. budget will not soon be balanced. But the spending is being diverted along different lines. The big tilt toward defense has a massive effect on technological development. It is not only war that is the mother of invention. War preparedness has some of the same effect—and we will look at ways to profit from it.

NEW RESEARCH
Every million dollars awarded in defense contracts contains at least a few thousands—more often a hundred thousand—for digging into technical problems. Some is for basic research into areas that were not even imagined before; some for practical research into making new things work well. The two combined will soon reverse a horrifying fact that you may not be aware of: The major part of new U.S. patents has been issued to foreigners, especially the Japanese, Germans, and Russians for some years. We were heading toward a situation where we would have to pay royalties to the outside world for the right to use most of the processes operating in our own country. This is about to end.

AUTOMOTIVE BREAKTHROUGHS
How can I be sure of that? The automotive industry, to take one of the giant examples, is readying a revolution as great as Henry Ford's. American companies are developing supereconomy cars that will get 60 and more miles to the gallon. They will be smaller and weigh less than half of the compact cars of the present day, but they will move a lot of people to where they want to go. This development—plus a great conversion to coal and changes in homeheating—will reinvigorate suburban neighborhoods that started to dwindle as fuel costs soared.

Two major results that will open up innumerable profit opportunities are expected: One is a wave of new construction; the other a persistent glut of oil and gas in the world. All of the discoveries of new petroleum reserves in Mexico, Alaska,

Indonesia, North Sea, Central America, and many other areas will show an oversupply that has been hidden by America's old insistence on burning it ostentatiously. Now the other extreme—long feared by the Saudi Arabians as something that might lessen the value of their huge reserves—will change the whole picture. I do not foresee that energy prices will drop anywhere near the old levels, but they will move downward while other prices trend upward—making the true *relative* cost of energy cheaper than anyone envisions now.

ELECTRONIC REVOLUTION

Microelectronics, to take another example of technical revolution, is about to change the way that innumerable things are done today. And the investment avenues this opens up are many and wide. As stated by The Organization for Economic Cooperation and Development: "The electronics complex will be the main pole around which the productive structures of advanced industrial societies will be reorganized." In simpler language, the statement means that tiny electronic circuits are now in the process of *replacing millions of human hands as ways to get things made.*

You probably think of microelectronics only as something that runs computers and grinds out a mass of data, but it is also being adapted to making products. Not surprisingly the Japanese are near the forefront of this development, and some of their innovations have severely jolted their American competitors. But while the race goes on for world dominance in devices that could add up to $25 billion in business around the world in the next couple of years, the United States is far ahead in putting all of this to work in manufacturing *things.*

The new industry that has been created from this development is named CAD/CAM—meaning computer-aided design and computer-aided manufacturing. Its potential market is huge. The major manufacturing companies, and many smaller ones, that produce over a trillion dollars worth of goods yearly in the United States alone are prospective customers for its devices. The assistance that CAD/CAM can give them includes drastic cuts in labor costs and inventory costs, and a great boost in the reliability of product quality. Even if the new industry is still small—probably not yet $2 billion per year—its rate of growth is phenomenal.

The companies that make up this new field include three that devote themselves entirely to this activity:

- Computervision
- Autotrol
- Intergraph

A number of others, mostly larger companies, have gone into it with just part of their resources. These include Cross & Trecker and Cincinnati-Milacron, which have about 7% of their revenues from CAD/CAM. The giants, like IBM and General Electric, are up to more than $100 million in annual CAD/CAM sales, but that makes up only about 1% of total income, so the effect on stock values will not be great at any time soon.

TEXTILES, CLOTHING, SHOES

Just before writing this, I was having a week-long series of talks with most of the top officials of the European Common Market. In the course of our sessions, I was struck with how big a part of all world business is made up of things that people wear. Apart from food, wearables are the most common and essential products. So if I tell you that this vast field is in for a great overall change, you can imagine the effects on companies, stocks, and currencies this will create.

As Professors Howard Rush and Kurt Hoffman, of the University of Sussex, have pointed out, such lines as textiles, garments, and shoes could be in for a reverse revolution that will undo the shift that had favored the developing countries for some years. More than half of the manufactured goods made by Hong Kong, Taiwan, South Korea, and the developing nations have prospered because the great supply of human labor enabled them to undercut the prices of the advanced countries. But now automation of textile manufacturing is racing ahead.

I have learned that the American textile industry is spending at the rate of $2 billion yearly on new equipment. Its labor-saving potential is shown by a new spinning mill that recently opened where just 95 persons in a single plant will produce as much as three plants with a workforce of 435 did formerly.

Similarly, the inexpensive production of garments in developing countries will be put into the shade by electronically controlled laser cutting which enables one person to do the work of ten. The making of television sets and other consumer electronics is being done with a 50% drop in the workforce. And even the making of the electronic circuits themselves is about to be automated—labor-saving devices being turned out faster and cheaper by still other labor-saving devices.

The Dark Side of Progress

The potentially horrendous problems that can be created by all this are apparent. I expect to see productivity at a rate that far outstrips the market's ability or desire to buy all these goods; poor nations going backward into greater poverty and defaulting on their huge debts to our major banks; massive unemployment that could lead to a violent backlash—even to the possibility of workers angrily destroying machines. These are part of the reason for my conviction that you must protect your investments against eventual bad times.

But even while all these dilemmas are building up, we will see many problems of the last twenty years apparently easing. The leading nations, with their grip on high technology, will reassert themselves, ending the years of apologetic subservience to former colonies that felt able to dictate terms to their old masters. The United States, because of its size, its massive capital, its enormous companies (remember that IBM alone accounts for more than half of the worldwide sale of the vital computer industry that will dominate all other industries), and its established lead will be the acknowledged master of this new technological revolution. This is far from being unalloyed good news for the long run. But what it tells us is that things are going to look a lot different.

And this means: *Don't dwell on the past performance of any type of investment.* The commonest questions I get revolve around the notion that what has been thriving in the past few years will be the best thing to bet on for the future. Salesmen of all kinds push this. One says, "Real estate has gone up by 10% per year. So buy real estate." Another points out, "Gold rose from $200 to $850, then came way down. That proves it's ready for a new rise." Still another says, "Diamonds have appreciated even more than gold, so invest in diamonds." Then there are collectibles—art, French furniture, Chinese porcelain. Each one with higher percentage gains than the one before. Isn't that proof of what is best to buy? And the stock market lagged during much of that time. Doesn't that tell you to stay out of stocks? Such thinking, natural as it is, is the sure road to financial ruin.

New Paths for Old Investments

The U.S. dollar, foreign currencies, gold, silver, other commodities, stocks, options—each will base its new path on a different set of conditions. Not always predictable paths, but many *are* foreseeable. It is definitely possible to identify the fundamental facts that will enable you to come out well ahead, to outperform even many professional money managers. Because, if you are willing to put some time and thought into it, you have advantages over the professionals, who are hampered by the need to buy in large quantities. They drive the prices up for themselves, then find they are stuck in markets that will tumble if they move to sell. I will show you how you can go into small situations and diversify enough to be fairly safe—whatever happens.

3

Your Twin Goals: More Profit, Less Risk

We are no longer in a world where being a prudent planner means finding one good investment and holding on to it indefinitely. People looking for financial advice usually ask me, "What should I buy?" in a way that reveals how anxious they are for one simple answer. It would be nice if I could just give one neat instruction: "Buy X Corp. stock," "Buy Krugerrands," or "Buy municipal bonds." But that would be dangerously wrong.

If you are really serious about achieving the twin goals of *making financial progress* and *having financial security,* you have to recognize that *these goals lie in two different directions*. Aiming for both means having at least two plans in motion at any one time. Not just any two, but two that are carefully chosen to complement each other. That is the bare minimum.

I have included in this book details of over a dozen separate trading or investing methods which can be combined in many ways to form a financial strategy that will best suit your situation, goals, temperament . . . and the two-step economic movement I see ahead of us. Any number of variations are possible, resulting in different mixtures of potential risks and rewards. But the basic idea will be the same in all cases: The blending of two or more approaches that give you both profitability and security.

First, Your Balance Sheet

As with any other serious plan, this one must start with a clear understanding of where you are right now. The first step is to make a balance sheet, listing all you own and all you owe. You don't have to be precise to the last dollar for our present purposes because you are looking for an overall picture, not for a fine focus. Just list an approximation of the present value of your assets:

- Cash in savings accounts, certificates, money market funds, Treasury bills.
- Cash value of your insurance.
- Cash value of any pension or profit-sharing plans.
- Market value of your home and any other real estate you own.
- Market value of stocks and bonds.
- Estimated worth of any share you have in a business venture.

Most balance sheets of this kind also list the value of autos, home furnishings, and other personal property. I do not recommend including these for present purposes because any asset that is needed in order to maintain a decent standard of living is not going to be sold to make investments. Although the same might be said of your home, I suggest including it because its equity value might be mortgaged for the purpose of putting cash into a more productive investment.

On the liability side, list everything you owe:

- Current bills
- Installment loans
- Other bank loans
- Mortgages
- Taxes

If you stop at this point, as many financial planners do, the balance sheet tells you nothing about where these assets may take you in the future. The difference between total assets and total liabilities is your "net worth." But how significant is this

in reality? Since you are not going to liquidate all your holdings as of today, this picture can be misleading if it is not
followed by something more. It is like a quick snapshot,
whereas life—like a movie—goes on to change that frozen
pose into a whole series of forms.

Two True Stories

Two calls that I received during the past week from persons
asking for advice will show you why a simple balance sheet
can be so inadequate in volatile times like these. One call was
from a man of about fifty. He said, "I have some cash savings
that were about enough to buy a new car when I put them into
the bank a few years ago. Now, even after earning interest,
they are just about enough for a down payment on a new car."
The other call was from a widow who had thought herself very
secure. But, she said, "Quite a bit of my money was in some
high-grade bonds that were supposed to be perfectly safe. I
guess the companies *are* safe. They pay the interest promptly
and there is no fear of default. But . . . the cash value of those
bonds has fallen along with the whole bond market. So if I sold
now, I would have only 60% as much money as I thought I
had."
  Such experiences are not only common; they are almost
universal these days. But the fact that values can change so
rapidly in these times does not have to be a bleak one. The
worth of some things can move *up* just as rapidly. A well-
chosen group of investments can mean that you are not locked
into a poor or mediocre position. While the balance sheet you
make up today can dwindle if too much of it is in cash-type
assets that lose their buying power, it can also expand beautifully if it is converted into investments that have the capacity
to grow. So we come to the second, and by far the more important, step in our assessment of how well you are fixed.

Second, The Key Questions

If we were having a personal talk, I might ask you: "Looking
at the assets you own, how much ability do they have to mul-

tiply in value?" After you have given it a thought, you will know whether your investments are of the kind that have at least the *potential* for rapid expansion. Take an exaggerated example, if a large part of what you own were in stock options or in highly volatile glamor stocks, you would be able to say, "My net worth *could* multiply by eight or ten times in a matter of months." If more normal growth stocks made up much of your holdings, the chance of a healthy expansion would still be there, even though less exciting. But if your assets are mostly in Treasury bills, you know they have almost no chance of great growth.

On the other hand, this last type of investment would allow you to answer very positively my next question: "How *secure* and *stable* are these assets of yours?" The volatile stocks that rated so high in that first instance would add very little to your sense of security.

And finally my third question: "How *flexible* are your investments?" That would require a little more explaining. How fast and how practical would it be for you to convert some of your assets into other forms in order to meet sudden needs or to get into more lucrative investments? With a little reflection, you would soon know whether your balance sheet is a very "liquid" one that makes it simple for you to move or it locks you into a position that will involve effort and cost to break out of.

New View of Your Prospects

Those three criteria—Multiplying Power, Stability, and Flexibility—add up to the most important way to judge your financial condition. A hefty balance sheet with large assets is always desirable, of course. But seen in this new light, a relatively modest *net worth* figure can sometimes point to a financial future that is brighter than that of a person with larger holdings in a less dynamic form.

Now look more carefully at all your investments and measure them against each of these standards:

MULTIPLYING POWER. As a general rule, the safer an investment is, the less chance of gain it offers. So the assets that have the greatest profit potential usually involve considerable risk. In each of the financial tactics discussed in this book, I will indicate how much risk of loss is involved as opposed to how great a possible reward is offered. But don't worry about risk just now. Consider only where your own investments fit into the range of profit potential . . . and how highly leveraged they are—meaning how much chance there is for small amounts to grow rapidly. Starting with the most dynamic investments and working down to the lowest in growth potential, the list goes this way:

- Commodities
- Stock options
- Penny stocks
- Listed stocks selling at low prices
- Highly mortgaged rental real estate
- Corporate bonds and bond funds
- Blue chips and other top-grade stocks
- Gold coins
- Gold-mine shares
- Silver coins
- Diamonds and other gemstones
- Utilities stocks
- U.S. Treasury bills and other cash savings

I suggest that you write the round figures of how much you have next to each appropriate item on the above list. This will quickly tell you whether your investments have some chance, a slight chance, or none at all of soon making you a great deal better off than you are today. There is no exact level of multiplying power that can be defined as "correct." But it is clearly *incorrect* to have only the assets that are at the bottom of the list.

Most people in their earning years should have about half of their assets in the first seven positions shown. In an inflationary world at least a portion of your holdings must be capable of growing in order to keep your buying power from receding.

STABILITY. The ability of your investments to resist unforeseeable setbacks is essential. NO amount of potential gain is any good without a safety net that ensures you against a disastrous fall. There is an unscientific, but somehow inevitable, law that goes, "If anything can possibly go wrong, it *will* go wrong." To bet against this law is foolhardy.

You will notice that the amount of security offered by each type of investment listed below is roughly opposite to the growth power indicated on the first list. But the word "roughly" is enormously significant in this case. The two lists do not run exactly opposite to each other. This means that a few items offer a better ratio of risk to reward than the others do. Precious metals, gold stocks, and listed stocks selling at low prices are the most favorable examples. Highly mortgaged real estate is just the opposite—its risks will be somewhat greater in proportion to its potential reward.

Keep in mind that the following list is not designed to show the conventional type of "steadiness" which is based on preserving certain dollar figures. For, in that case, cash and Treasury bills would naturally be at the head of the list. But as the caller in one of my examples found out, his "secure" savings were a very unsafe way to prepare for a future of rising prices. So you should not think strictly in dollar terms as you study the safety of your holdings, but rather in terms of changed buying power. And that range of true stability—going from the steadiest to the least reliable—reads like this:

- Gold coins
- Silver coins
- Utilities stocks
- U.S. Treasury bills and other cash savings
- Gold-mine shares
- Blue chips and other top-grade stocks
- Listed stocks selling at low prices
- Corporate bonds and bond funds
- Diamonds and other gemstones
- Highly mortgaged real estate
- Commodities
- Penny stocks
- Stock options

Here again, as in the case of multiplying power, there is no exact right or wrong about what you should have. Aiming for the highest possible degree of safety is not wise if it also shackles you to virtually no gains. As each one of these investments is taken up in the appropriate chapter, I will indicate ways to deal in that asset with minimum risk. And in all the methods that I suggest I will prepare you to have a fall back position where nothing that happens could seriously harm your living standard, or leave you without the means to recover your momentum and invest again.

For now, however, simply compare your present holdings with the positions on this list, and determine about how much of a cushion your investments provide. Are you reasonably safe from an unexpected setback? If at least a third to a half of all you own is capable of resisting any recession or market reversal that you can envision, you probably have as much security as any investor should hope for—*assuming that you are at the earning time of your life*. As long as new money will be coming along to replace any that might be lost, it is wise to take calculated risks for the sake of trying to make major progress. *But if you are retired or near it* and you have to live on rather limited funds, a good three-fourths of all you have should be in the lowest-risk investments occupying the first five places on this list.

FLEXIBILITY. In its simplest form, this means how easily each of your assets can be converted and used to move into a different category. Considerable flexibility is essential because the economic churning which is ahead will make it very imprudent to put investments away and leave them untouched. Cash, Treasury bills, nearly all stocks, bond funds, gold and silver coins, and commodities are all very "liquid." An order to sell them can be given one day and the proceeds made available for your use within a few hours to five days, at most. In some cases—savings certificates, for instance—there may be some penalty for liquidating quickly, but not enough to tie you up if some overriding need for the money develops. On the other hand, bonds that you have bought on your own (not through a fund) may take some time to sell, unless you want to make a real sacrifice. Diamonds and other gemstones are very difficult to dispose of quickly without considerable discount from the quoted market values. And real estate takes longest of all to turn into hard cash.

As you look at your investments from this angle, think not only of whether they could conceivably be sold, but also whether it is practical for *you* to do so. Some investments that are flexible for one person are not so for someone else. A very successful investor, for example, has most of his net worth tied up in millions of dollars of IBM stock that he began acquiring for just a few dollars per share many years ago. This wealthy man, however, has such enormous gains on his stock that his tax liability on any sale keeps him locked in. Other people who had bought the shares around their present levels fairly recently could sell them at once without the problem.

Investments that have a great spread between the buying and selling prices can be problems also. They *can* be sold at once, but anyone who tries to do so may take a bad beating for his haste. This is often true of rare coins, stamps, art objects, and the like. If you want to buy such an item, its value is put at, let us say, $10,000. If you want to resell it, you have to wait and find a collector who is willing to pay top dollar for it. Or you may resell it to a dealer, perhaps the same one who sold it to you. But now he will pay no more than $8,000. All of this may be quite fair, considering his operating expenses and the time he will have to hold it. But from your point of view the article is not a flexible part of your financial assets.

Of course, you have to assign very low flexibility to anything like a profit-sharing plan connected with your work. If you are only a year or so away from retirement, it begins to be almost like cash in your pocket. But at earlier times, anything that you cannot use without quitting your job hardly deserves to be part of the current picture at all.

At least 50% of all you own should be quite flexible. If that is not so, the pressure to make changes in that direction is urgent.

Once you have looked over your holdings from these three interlocking points of view, you may have quite a different feeling about your prospects. Any one of the lists may be a signal to you to start making prompt adjustments. For example, you may want to move some cash up to stocks or other items that are high on List No. 1, or to convert some real estate or bond fund holdings to utilities stocks or precious metals.

Then as you study the possible investments that I discuss in this book, you can consider each one not only on its own merits, but also from the standpoint of how it relates to your overall picture. If you have found that there is nothing at all capable of dynamic growth in your present portfolio, I suggest that you give a little more attention than you normally would to such subjects as stocks, commodities, and stock options. You need not plunge with much of your capital. But it *is* the new kind of prudency of our era to move toward investments with more ability to multiply. Coupled with what you have just learned about the ways to preserve stability and the "safety net" approach that I will stress along the way, your investment portfolio can be improved and pointed in the *directions* of progress. The odd plural form is intentional, for if I had to choose a single word that best ensures your financial future, I would say—DIVERSIFY.

4

Why You Must Diversify

You already know what I think American and other advanced economies are going to do—first expand unevenly for several years, then get into serious trouble. But you should know that many scenarios different from my own have been envisioned by economic analysts of great standing. One of the most striking examples of how widely the expert views can vary has been set out by the economists of Morgan Guaranty Trust Company, of New York, who admit that at least three outlooks seem equally likely to them. I am going to summarize these possibilities here because they will help you to realize that just picking one investment and pinning your whole future to it is unwise.

First, there is a "base case" in which real economic growth in the industrialized world (not just the United States) recovers to an annual rate of 3% and world trade grows about 5% annually. Real oil prices would rise at about that same rate. And inflation would be about 9% to 10% yearly—causing interest rates to be around 12%–13%.

Second, there is a more optimistic case that assumes the major nations will conserve energy enough to curb the rise in oil prices. This would leave more spending and investing power to be used for faster economic growth and more world trade. It would also send inflation lower, and interest rates down along with it.

Last, there is a pessimistic scenario, wherein oil prices would surge in 1983–1984, prompting a burst of even heavier inflation, a new jump in interest rates, and sending economic growth into a tailspin.

Without taking you through the effects that each case would have on all the separate parts of our society, I want to mention what would happen to the deficits of the poorest nations—one of the world's greatest and most explosive problems. Our banking system has loaned many billions of dollars to those countries and lives in hope that the loans will not go completely bad, with possible effects on the solvency of our own banks. In the optimistic case given above, the debts of such countries would grow by only 8½% a year, which is considered very tolerable. In the worst case, however, the debts would speed up by 32% per year, meaning that banks would probably be unable or unwilling to keep giving them funds—and that the old loans might have to be declared in default. You don't have to be an economist to judge how much more desirable an investment in gold coins, for example, would be in the last case than in the first.

So a great many leading experts are saying, in effect, that the world economy could go pretty well, very well, or abominably in the next few years. I have already stated my view of the most likely outcome; but I will give you a set of strategies that will win in *any* foreseeable situation—even one that differs from my forecast. Again, I urge you to avoid clinging to any preset notion or losing investment for that is one of the commonest and the most costly mistakes of all.

Dividing Your Capital

Your investment capital, whether it consists of just a few thousand dollars or goes into six or seven figures, must be divided in a number of ways. It should be put into several types of assets. I am devoting little space to urban real estate, antiques, and collectibles because their prices have become so inflated in recent years that even after current declines, only isolated opportunities now exist. If you are an expert in any of these fields, and find a chance to own a certain corner property, antique Chinese export bowl, or rare stamp that you feel is certain to appreciate regardless of what the economy does, fine. But this is different from regarding real estate or collectibles in general as a good and liquid form of investment.

The assets I will cover also require careful selection, but are more likely to be supported by a general trend so that any prudent person without specific expertise should be able to make wise choices. These include:

- Stocks or mutual funds.
- Bonds, money market funds, and savings certificates.
- Precious metals.
- Nonprecious metal and minerals.
- Stock options.
- Commodities.

If you have very large amounts of capital free for investment, there is good reason to put some into each of the above. Over a period of time, all are apt to prosper in varying degrees. By balancing the amount put into each category, you can maximize your gain.

Not surprisingly, such diversity is harder to attain for the small investor; and especially so for the average retiree. Harder, but not impossible. He must move more delicately, but he can still own several of these assets. And to be really diversified, he has to *divide the amounts into categories that will behave differently in each of the possible scenarios*.

For example, when interest rates go into another of those upward spirals, it is not enough to say, "I have 25% of my funds in the form of cash savings." The question is: "Are they in a form that will keep up with interest-rate increases or are they locked to a fixed figure?" This will be explained very simply later. Here it is only intended to get you accustomed to the general principle of diversification.

To continue with our example, you can save cash in a fixed-interest certificate or a fund whose rate varies daily. Most people think they are similar. In fact, they are as opposite as the two poles. An investor who is locked into a 1-year Trea-

sury bill or a 2½-year certificate at, say, 11% will feel miserable if rates move up to 14, 18, or 20%. He must either pay a
penalty in order to switch—perhaps at the very wrong
moment—or keep accepting an outmoded income on that part
of his capital. Meanwhile, the investor who put his cash into
a money market fund is beaming—his returns are compounding at higher and higher rates. But who knows when they will
start down? He will then wish that he had converted the fund
to a certificate exactly at the peak point.

Averaging Is Better than Timing

Forget any dream of ideal timing. You might accidentally
achieve it once in five or six business cycles. Not even the
professionals do any better, nor do they waste much time in
trying. The best of them who are managing for *results* aim for
the highest possible average rate. That is achieved by playing
both sides of the street—splitting the cash portion of your
assets into at least two types of savings.

You will find my specific advice on what you can do with
your cash to ensure that it will grow regardless of market
conditions in Chapter 11. Briefly stated, you should put half
into a money market fund and the other half into a bond fund.
If interest rates rise, the sum total of ups and downs in the two
funds will give you a very good *average* rate—about as good
as the professionals manage and far better than most lay-
men do.

But what happens if rates start to drop? You are in an even
better position. The return on your money market fund starts
sliding, true. But the interest income on your bond fund,
being fixed, stays quite constant. AND . . . the *value* of the
bonds in that fund rises. Any time you want to, you can shift
out of that fund and take the increased value of your principal
as a capital gain. Whether you sell out of the bond fund entirely or only shift part of it depends on your tax situation and
your guess about the economy's future. Either way, your total
return on the cash portion of your holdings will be excellent.

As a general rule, you will achieve the maximum gains by

always leaning against the prevailing wind—that is, whenever you get new cash to invest, put more of it into the bond fund after the rates have been high for some time and bonds are low. This may seem an unattractive thing to do, but it leaves you with more room for upside movement a few months hence. As you do some of this in actual practice, you will get "the feel of the market," and your performance will improve. You will notice, for example, that really large swings in rates generally last longer than most analysts expect, or say they expect. (It is not at all certain that some of these experts don't mislead the business reporters by talking down the price of things whenever they intend to be buyers.) So you don't move your cash out of the bond fund just one or two weeks after it turns upward. You wait for a capital gain that is substantial enough to be worth the switch and the tax you will owe on it. Besides, your main goal with this part of your assets is a long-term one. You want to keep some of your cash in the fixed-rate market as well as in the one that moves daily, unless a huge move in one or the other of these makes it obvious that the pendulum will soon have to swing the other way.

Dividing Your Hedges

Similarly, the money you set aside to invest in inflation hedges should be divided. With just a few thousand dollars you can own some gold coins, some South African gold-mine shares, and some silver coins.

Why do I suggest all this fuss instead of just owning gold coins? Because your coins will do well in a highly inflationary time, but they yield no income and can also fall back sharply at times when interest rates get so high that they attract money away from gold. The better gold-mine stock will pay a high rate of income and still give you a hold on the gold price because of the reserves of ore they have underground. There is also a balancing element in the coins and stocks—any political violence in South Africa could drop the value of the gold stocks for a time, but it would tend to raise the price of the metal itself, since the supply from Africa might be diminished.

Silver coins, although their general path seems to follow that of gold, will sometimes do better and sometimes worse than gold. This will be explained in detail when we talk more about silver. When the coins are bought with the timing that is suggested in that chapter, they can outperform gold and act as something of a hedge against your gold investment.

There is also an interesting form of coin investment that has sometimes been called "absolutely risk-free," although this is open to argument. It is the saving of brand-new rolls of U.S. coins. When kept in that original form, they tend to gain collector value over the years. The increase was very substantial, of course, when U.S. coins were made of silver and precious metals climbed in price. But even after 1964 and the introduction of coins with far less intrinsic value, these new rolls of pennies, nickels, dimes, and quarters have shown good gains.

Since they are U.S. legal tender, they are sure to be worth at least their face value; hence, the claim that there is "NO risk." But holding an asset that pays no yield can be a loss, if it fails to appreciate in value, because it means foregoing the interest that might have been earned.

The chance that these coin rolls *will* gain value depends on U.S. inflation. If it climbs sharply, as I expect, almost any collectible of this kind is very likely to move up strongly in price. So new U.S. coin rolls *are* a hedge against the one evil that poses the chief threat. And whether or not you choose to think that they are absolutely risk-free, they are certainly one of the lowest-risk investments anywhere. These coin rolls can be bought at your own bank for their exact face value, of course. They may not always be available, but any friendly teller or bank officer will try to find some for you. When you want to resell, ask several coin dealers how much they are offering. And compare their quotes with advertisements you will find in one of the magazines that deal with coins and collectibles.

Balancing Your Stocks

I have left for last the most important category for diversification. Your common stocks have to be selected in a way that takes into account not only the coming inflation—the kind of products and companies that can ride through it best—but also various swings in social attitudes on anti-pollution, on amount of leisure activities, on home and office construction, and so on.

Let's look at an example of how this works in actual practice: You have $40,000 worth of common stocks, and as you look over the portfolio you realize that nearly all of them are dependent on a great improvement in the energy situation—a lowering in the cost of fuels. They include General Motors (which could suffer if people are forced to drive less), Johns Manville (whose sales of insulating materials will slide if high fuel costs prevent the construction of more suburban homes), and Holiday Inns (whose occupancy rates and profits will decline if there is less tourism). You like the individual prospects for each of the companies you own, but you don't want to be hurt if their stocks should lose value because of an outside factor, such as an OPEC decision to cut oil production and send petroleum prices soaring again.

I suggest several ways you can diversify to protect yourself. The most straightforward one is to buy long-term "put" options on these same stocks—a form of insurance which is covered in a separate chapter. You could also achieve a balance by selling about a third of the total value of these stocks and investing the cash in the stocks of companies that stand to benefit if fuel prices rise. Companies that deal with nuclear power are in that position because as conventional fuels get more costly, the nuclear approach comes closer to being economical. You could buy the makers of nuclear reactors, like Babcock & Wilcox or Westinghouse or you could buy South African mines, like Harmony and Hartebeestfontein. These have uranium and they also have gold, which almost invariably rises on the inflationary news of an oil-price increase.

If you are a young investor who is struggling with the costs of raising a new family and who has only $8,000 for stock investments, you should take a different approach. You might put $5,000 into a mutual fund with a solid record of performance in years of economic expansion, such as the Templeton Fund, or one of the Keystone or Merrill Lynch funds. Then you could put the other $3,000 into a fund that specializes in South African mining shares, like Precious Metal Holdings, or into one of the several funds that stress energy stocks. You might very well end up making money on both chunks of your capital because the growth funds are sometimes operated deftly enough to forge ahead a little, even during difficult times when your $3,000 diversification will be booming. But even if not, you should move through any rough period with your capital positioned to expand nicely later on, when you will presumably need it most for your children's college costs.

If you are a retiree who has total capital of $60,000 in addition to a pension and social security checks, you may feel that you should not have common stocks at all. Only by getting an assured interest income from savings certificates or Treasury bills, are you augmenting your yearly cash intake enough to live moderately well. To risk any of it on the ups and downs of the stock or bond markets seems foolhardy. But you *can* tap their capital gains possibilities without undue risk, if you diversify properly. The technique I mentioned above, of putting half the cash into a money market fund and the other half into a bond fund, will bring you the same amount of income and still offer the chance of capital gains on the latter portion of your money. Or you can put that half into utilities stocks or top quality gold-mine stocks. The income will be at least as high as you get from a money fund or a savings certificate, and there is a good chance that the value will trend upward over the years.

Safeguarding Your Capital

Just as with interest rates and precious metals, there are ways to assure yourself that almost any investment will take you to higher ground. I will restate this principle in various ways throughout this book.

- If you trade stock *options*, have some "puts"—betting on a decline—as well as the more common and optimistic "call" options.
- If you put money into high-yield Mexican peso savings

certificates, consider selling short some peso futures in order to be insured against a possible Mexican devaluation.
- If you trade commodities, try to be in several types that do not always move in a single direction. A low-cost diversification of this kind can be set up to lessen the risk in almost every investment. It may at first seem to be complicated and dangerous business, but if you examine it closely, you will realize that it can be the opposite—a solid way to safeguard the bulk of your capital.

As Lawrence H. Heim, a remarkably sound financial counselor based in Portland, Oregon, often reminds his clients: Remember, it is even more important to avoid losing money than it is to make money.

5

Investing versus Speculating

Knowing the difference between an investment and a speculation is vital to your plan for early gains and long-range protection against the troubles of the later 1980's. The distinction depends largely on *you*. Like the saying that beauty is in the eye of the beholder, investment is in the mind of the investor. *Your* intention helps determine the nature of the deal.

I suggest the following simple definitions as a guide to the main points:

- An investment is the purchase of something that is well established, apparently safe from the risk of *major* loss, and offering considerably more chance of gaining value than of losing value over a period of three or more years—*and which you plan to hold for at least that long.*
- A speculation is the purchase of something that could be either safe or risky, that you think will gain very rapidly, *and that you hope to resell for a quick profit.*

Going on that basis, a large, supposedly solid piece of real estate, stock, or any other prime asset may actually be a speculation. Suppose you are offered a chance to buy a share in a real estate syndicate that plans to take over a large apartment building and resell it as condominium dwellings. The hope is to make the conversion as rapidly as possible. If all goes smoothly, your $5,000 share can easily double in value and may gain even more. But if tenant resistance or objections by local housing authorities should intervene, the plan might drag or fail altogether. This is a speculation.

By the same definition, a low-cost item may be an investment. Suppose you hear of the stock of a small manufacturing company that has been selling between $6 and $9 a share for years, and you are also aware that it plans to introduce a new product which seems very promising to you. The decision to put $800 into it can be an investment if you plan to pass up any chance for quick gain and to hold on for the very long pull. The difference is between hoping to resell soon for a $2,000 gain or being willing to wait years for potential stock splits and increases to give you a six-figure stake in a new Xerox or Polaroid.

Weighing Risk and Reward

There is confusion about this basic subject because most people have the impression that speculation is bad and investment is good. That is not so. This particular purchase would still be an investment if the company's performance were to disappoint, but it would have been a bad one. The financial world is full of poor investors and rich speculators. Investors who take poor risks do badly. Speculators who take well-calculated risks do well. Although the words seem contradictory, there *are* prudent or even conservative gamblers.

I hope you will always recognize that everything carries some risk. There is nothing that you can buy, lock up in a safe, and be absolutely sure of selling at a profit any moment you choose. Some things are certain to be worth more in the course of time, but they may have erratic periods when it would be unfortunate if you had to sell them. So, since there is risk in all things, it is the *degree* of risk, versus the possible reward, that has to be measured.

Anyone who repeatedly goes into situations where the potential reward is greater than the risk will come out ahead, assuming that he has the resources to ride out any reasonable number of setbacks until the favorable odds begin to work in his benefit.

Taking some specific types of assets, I will explain which ones normally lend themselves to being used as speculations and which are more suitable as investments:

STOCKS

Let's begin with stocks, which present the most evenly divided opportunities for either investment or speculation. Investing in stocks or trading in them are two entirely different activities, which is why I have devoted separate chapters to the techniques for profiting from each method.

The stock market is full of *unwilling* investors—they bought a stock as speculators, saw it fall instead of rise, then grimly held on, hoping to get their money back. This is the worst of all possible worlds—to tie up capital in something that has ceased to be either a speculation or a true investment in the sterile hope of "getting even." A splendid book called *The Sophisticated Investor,* written by the late Burton Crane many years ago, had the only rule I know for completely avoiding this fate: If you buy something because you expect it to go up right away and it doesn't, sell it. That doesn't mean to wait for a little better price, to examine all the possible reasons why it hasn't done as you expected, or—most fatal of all errors—"to watch it for a while." It means to sell at once. Period.

Blue chip stocks are sometimes the unwisest of all gambles. It depends, of course, on the time, the price, and especially on what else is available for purchase. Very often, the chance of a blue chip's rising is far less than that of a cheaper and less recognized issue, while the likelihood of a decline is every bit as great as that of the lesser stock. Time and again, a general stock market drop proves the old maxim that when things go badly the baby gets thrown out with the bath water. When the averages dive sharply, General Motors and DuPont are apt to lose very nearly the same percentage of their value as a smaller established company trading at $15 a share. But on an upswing, the latter can triple in value while the blue chips add only 20% or 30%.

This has been demonstrated repeatedly. When the market fell in 1948 and in 1960, almost every major stock you can name tumbled at least as much as the Dow Jones Average— General Electric, Westinghouse, Kennecott, Phelps Dodge, ALCOA, and so on. Meanwhile, a representative group of stocks in the $10 to $20 price range—not new, unstable companies, but firms doing $50, $100, $200 million in annual business— fell by about the same percentage. But as soon as the recovery came, these stocks shot up 2½ times as fast as the blue chips.

More astonishing is the fact that these traditional invest- ments are sometimes poor gambles even in absolute terms— not merely relative to other assets. They actually have more potential risk than possible reward. It is not necessary to look for the nightmare stories of huge companies that made the first page with their plunges—Chrysler, Ford, Con Edison, and Penn Central. Many others that are nowhere near the point of collapse are more likely to fall 30 points than to rise 30 points within a given span of time. Despite all the talk there is among the most sophisticated money managers about "ratio of risk to reward"—often accompanied by algebraic equations—this elementary fact is frequently ignored.

The Importance of Fashion

Why, I have been asked, should anyone even consider blue chip stocks if their ratio of reward to risk is not as good as some other securities offer? The answer lies in the fashion of the times. There was a period through the 1960's and into the early 1970's when stock market psychology pushed nearly all issues far too high. The glamor stocks that sold for 100 and 200 times annual earnings were, of course, the most wildly over- priced. But at least a canny *speculator* who bought one of those with his eyes open for $75 a share might be rewarded by passing it on to someone else quickly for $90 a share. If he did it with the resolve to sell out at $70 in case of a reversal, he was acting with a certain kind of logic, balancing the hope of a $15 gain against the risk of a $5 loss. But there were managers of large funds, handling other people's savings and pension money, who kept plowing it into Eastman Kodak, Dow Chemical, and such other blue chips at 25 times annual earnings and more. Why? No possible combination of income and capital gain could make that a prudent gamble. They had just stopped thinking and kept going on the premise that their job was to invest in "quality stocks." So at such a time, blue chips made no sense at all.

Beginning in 1973, and then continuing for some years, all these money managers, and then the bruised and battered general public, sold the blue chips. The fund managers had finally realized, for one thing, that they had too much cash in a few main assets. Even if they genuinely liked certain stocks—Kodak is an example—they did not want that much of their total holdings in those items. Their selling inevitably pushed the prices far down.

Now, as I write this, some of those quality stocks really *are* good buys. Selling at seven, eight, or ten times annual earnings, stocks of such companies have a very good chance of doubling in value. They still are not apt to show the percentage gains of lower-priced shares, and they do not move fast enough to make them attractive speculations. But when evaluated on a total-return basis—adding up the substantial dividends they pay and considering how much the overall amount will grow if those dividends are used to buy more of the same stock—they can be good *investments*.

BONDS

Bonds were once an investment. Truly an investment for they carried an assured income at a certain rate, and when purchased at an advantageous moment, there was the chance of some capital gain. If, for example, the economy had become a bit too sluggish and the government wanted to speed it up, it would usually reduce interest rates a little, which raised the value of existing bonds. Now that we have seen interest rates of such incredible proportions, those movements seem trifling in size, but they could create substantial profits, and with very low risk.

But bonds today are pure speculations. The money supply is already so huge that the value of the dollars to which bonds are tied can take large and sudden veers. Moreover, attempts to *control* the money supply are made in such big ways that the bond market tends to move up or down even more abruptly than the stock market.

Keep this clearly in mind in connection with any bonds you now hold, or with any commitments you may think about after reading the chapter on bonds. They should *NOT* be held as investments, however sound the issuing government, municipality, or corporation. It is a question not just of whether the payments will be met, but of what the value of money itself will be at those future dates.

UTILITIES

For those who have liked bonds as a way of getting high and steady income, I suggest that utilities stocks be considered as the alternate investment. Unlike bonds, they are bound to move up in price at some point because whatever the cost of fuels or the situation of the economy, the government commissions that regulate utilities rates have no choice but to let them rise whenever the companies lack enough profits to expand facilities and meet demand. So their stocks will pay reasonably high returns and their fluctuations will tend to have an upward bias, creating at least modest capital gains.

REAL ESTATE

For many years real estate has been very rewarding, both as a speculation and as an investment. Those who are in the trade or who devote enough time to make it a working hobby have often found special buying opportunities that lent themselves to quick and profitable turnovers. Any time a desirable house or other property can be bought from a hurried seller, this potential opens up. But now the problem of financing has become more important than mere price. So the would-be speculator must cope with the double task of scouring his area for bargain buys, while also making sure that the mortgage possibilities make a resale practical.

High interest rates are also getting in the way of the even greater returns that are possible from long-term investment. The leverage over a period of years makes these gains much greater than quick speculative ones, but only when the property is well and heavily mortgaged to begin with. On this basis, everything begins working in the buyer's favor: Inflation boosts the price; federal law creates a tax shelter; and the deductions for interest payments and annual depreciation are a major benefit to those in the middle-to-high tax brackets. If you have rental property that is purchased with a modest down payment, and that pays for all or most of the monthly carrying charges, all these advantages can produce a fine creation of capital.

But it is important to realize that high leverage works both ways. It can multiply losses just as it multiplies gains. We are now at a point where real estate values, after years of huge expansion, are vulnerable to the kind of shocks that can develop in our era. That is why I have previously rated highly mortgaged real property as relatively low in stability.

Note how different conditions are for investing in rental property today. You could once buy a $30,000 house with a $5,000 down payment, rent it for $275 a month, and actually have a little cash left over after covering monthly payments and occasional repairs. With a 9½% mortgage, you would have begun to build up considerable equity in just a few years, especially as the resale value also climbed.

Now the same house would cost $60,000 or more to buy. After a $10,000 down payment, you would have to meet monthly outlays of at least $450, which is more than you are likely to rent it for. And most important, your equity would grow very slowly for the 16% mortgage would divert so much of your payments to interest cost. Moreover, the chance of a big jump in resale value is much less likely at $60,000 than it was at $30,000.

My assessment of the future is that urban real estate values will continue to gain, but at a much slower pace than in the past. On a national average, they will move up just a little in 1983 and 1984, then more rapidly in the next several years—but less than the overall inflation rate. Working in their favor is the continued inflation, the large amounts of dollars now in savings certificates and money funds that could move to real estate, and the build-up of unsatisfied demand for housing during this troubled period. Working against them are the twin factors that prices have already gone so high and that all the new mortgaging devices that will be introduced to overcome present problems are going to dilute the owner's equity gains very substantially.

Mortgage rates of 16% or 18% are not going to make it permanently impossible for people to buy, as it may sometimes seem. These (or the new variable-rate mortgages that will amount to similar terms in the end) will really be a roundabout way for the *lender to take a major share of the equity gains*. This will leave less for the owner. After ten years of covering mortgage payments at these rates, he will find that even if property prices have moved up, his equity in a rental property has grown by only 12% or 14% a year. The 20% and higher rates of growth that prevailed in some earlier years will be divided between the buyer and the lender.

Real estate held on this basis is clearly an investment, but the arguments in its favor become borderline. The final rate of return, counting in the tax advantages, has to be weighed against the returns available from other investments.

Except for two specialized lines mentioned in the next chapter, I do not go into real estate in more detail because there are vast differences in various parts of the country, and even from one street to the next. No one can responsibly say—as with gold, options, stocks, and so on—that the entire category looks favorable or the reverse. For long periods the Sun Belt has boomed while the Midwest has slumped. But even within the Midwest, there are transport centers that have had remarkable surges. And there have also been times when over-speculation led to pullbacks in the Sun Belt's values. You have to know the trend within specific areas, sense the need and the availability of housing, and the business currents that will determine requirements for office and warehouse space. If you are willing to put the necessary effort into it, the chance for gain is still there.

But *never* buy any piece of property because "real estate has gone up so much for so long." That is, if anything, a reason for extra caution.

DIAMONDS

Diamonds, in my view, are neither good speculations for the near-term economic phase nor investments for the years beyond. I see no reason for giving them a place in any portfolio under present circumstances.

You will have noticed that I assigned a low rating to the ability of diamonds to multiply in value, which may have surprised you in view of the claims made about their enormous gains. Only very large stones of highest quality made the big percentage jumps that are spoken of. Most stones of ordinary color and normal size went up very much less. And they did very little for the individual persons who considered themselves investors because a diamond would have to move up by over 25% in value before the buyer could resell and *break even*. Only above that point would he start to profit.

The kinds of moves that lend themselves to wise speculation are therefore lacking. The long-term gains that go with investment are possible, but the prospect is not attractive, starting at today's prices. The truth is that diamonds went up as much as they did from a totally different cause: The great number of wealthy people who wanted to smuggle their fortunes across borders from such places as Rhodesia, Spain, France, and Iran made diamonds a much sought-after item for this purpose. People who stood to lose everything naturally put no price limits when they needed to buy a stone for hasty travel. So these were bid up to unrealistic heights. Anyone who buys at such points is paying a desperate person's price when he himself has no such need. And if he does it on the often-heard assurance that the DeBeers cartel can absolutely keep a floor under diamond prices because it was able to do so in earlier troubled times, he is overlooking a major point: DeBeers lost control of the market on the way up this time.

Prices were bid so high that any quieting of the demand could lead to hectic selling and ragged price movements. This is just what happened in 1981. Not even when DeBeers virtually stopped its own selling of investment-grade diamonds did the slide halt. There were already too many others with stones to dump onto the market.

On top of all this, much more diamond production in other parts of the world may overwhelm DeBeers' attempts at control. Some of the black African countries that formerly cooperated with the cartel show signs of breaking away. And a massive new producing area is being developed in the state of Western Australia, which could prove to be the world's largest producer. Although the Australians would presumably be anxious to avoid a big price decline, it seems unlikely that new understandings will be firm enough to maintain the old discipline. An item with so many question marks does not, in my opinion, count as a reasonable investment.

ANTIQUES AND COLLECTIBLES

There was a span of years in the 1970s when antique Chinese pottery had the biggest percentage jump in value compared with any other possible investment. The huge rise in price of Persian rugs is well known. So is the great move in various periods of antique furniture, not to mention the art works of great or less-than-great masters. If you happen to be an expert professional or hobbyist in some area of antiques and other collectibles, there may be ways for you to prepare for and benefit from some new move of this kind. But failing that, I would strongly oppose using collectibles as a way to add to your financial security.

In the first place, most of the astronomical figures you hear are misleading because it would not have been easily possible to *sell* at the high figure. That is the price you would have to pay if you were looking to buy. But all the middlemen's costs and profits would have trimmed considerably the real net gain. Second, it would be very rare for any group that enjoyed this surge so recently to get up a new momentum. The period of excitement probably brought out most of the potential buyers. After that, many of them actually became potential sellers, waiting for a chance to resell profitably. Even in the works of acknowledged great masters, many decades and sometimes centuries have usually lapsed between the periods of buying excitement and rising prices.

It is true that some beautifully crafted articles have one solid reason for holding their value—the skills and patience to produce them no longer exist, so that there is virtually no new supply. This can make such an article a good store of value, especially for a person on the move—such as a wealthy refugee from a troubled country. But the fickleness of popularity, the big problem of liquidating such goods at full value, and the already rather tired state of these markets should put collectibles off limits for your own money-making program.

COMMODITIES AND STOCK OPTIONS

The role of commodities and stock options is obvious if you refer to the definition earlier in this chapter. In most cases, you must rely on relatively short-term success in order to profit, so they are speculations when dealt in normally.

You will find later that I suggest conservative ways to put money into each of these areas. The methods are applicable to both economic stages that I am preparing you for. In the case of options, for example, I will describe two methods for generating income with virtually no risk. But for the purpose of this present division, the important thing is to recognize that ordinary forms of commodity trading or option buying should never involve money that is dedicated to investment.

Dividing Your Two Roles

Remember this one overriding essential: Each time you commit yourself to any deal, be sure you *know* whether you are thinking in speculative or investment terms. You can be both a speculator and an investor by dividing your capital into parts that are handled differently. But if you mingle the two roles, you will be almost sure to lose.

Understanding this distinction, coupled with the picture of your financial position that you gained from the lists suggested earlier, will give you the basis for making decisions on specific investments and speculations—balancing the two in ways that will give you more money to spend and much more money *to grow on*.

II

QUICK
PROFIT-BUILDING
STRATEGIES

6

Watching the Arabs for Profit Clues

"Which way is the big money moving?" is one of the questions that always fascinates financial people. Not because these huge flows of capital always prove to be going in the wise direction, but because the movement in itself causes certain investments to go up or down for a time.

Managers of mutual funds, insurance company investments, and pension funds have long been leaders in deciding which way each market would move. Now Arab investors have the potential to surpass them, for unlike the fund manager whose performance will be watched and second-guessed every quarter of the year by clients who want to see results, the wealthy Arab or the economic director of an Arab government can take a more independent view. Even if he is responsible to a ruling sheik, he can explain in person his reasons for making moves for long-range benefits. The salaried fund manager, however, is judged by a set of printed numbers, and tends to dilute his actions by moving cautiously. The Arab can and sometimes does act decisively enough to make a certain market move the way he has chosen. Almost everyone else is forced to guess which way the markets will go. Many Arab groups are able to MAKE the markets go their way.

This doesn't mean that the holders of billions of oil dollars are free from worry. When we say that the Arabs can make markets act as they want to, we mean they can do so *on the way in,* though not necessarily when the time comes to move out of a certain investment. The bullion dealers I talk with in New York, London, and Zurich tell me that a single Arab can cause the price of gold to skyrocket because just a billion or so of concentrated gold buying can send that small market soaring. But once it has climbed, what is the Arab investor to do? Unless he or some other enormously rich buyers keep bidding the price higher, it will drift or even fall. If he tries to sell out, the effect of that much selling will send the price down even faster than the buying sent it up.

Moreover, I know from personal talks that many Arabs feel straitjacketed by their vast wealth because none of the places they do try to put their investments looks entirely safe to them. They worry about holding too many U.S. dollars, too much of any one currency; they fret over their industrial investments, lest a severe depression in the West should shove some of the companies into bankruptcy. Even real estate, which is one of their favorite investments, gives them cause for concern whenever the people of that country make ominous sounds against "being taken over by the Arabs." They know, in other words, that their wealth in other countries could one day be expropriated and taken from them just as swiftly as they took over the holdings of Western oil companies a few years earlier.

So the Western-trained economic brains who are well paid to counsel the Arab governments and private millionaires have now begun to tell them, just as I have been telling you, to diversify as much as possible. They watch for opportunities to buy into assets that appear to be underpriced and can absorb large amounts of money without immediately zooming to an overpriced condition. Up to now, they have been only moderately successful in this. So when we talk of watching what the Arabs are doing, it is not because their investments have been clever but they *do* make things happen—things that the smaller investor can profit from without the shackles that great wealth imposes.

Lessons the Arabs Learned

Start with a look at the checkered history of Arab investments in the West, dating back to the time in 1973–1974 when they set the price of oil soaring for the first time. They were badly advised, and they put considerable sums into the U.S. stock market, just when a long bull market had ended and a six-year decline was beginning. There were many technical factors to show the market was overpriced and tired, many fundamental facts of inflation and bloated money supplies, which were grossly worsened by the oil price increase.

It should have been foreseeable. If anyone should have known which way the Western economies were headed, it was the Arabs—they helped send them into a tailspin. For an oil producer to invest in the health of the West at that time was like an arsonist investing his money in fire insurance companies. Anyway, they did it and, of course, lost heavily. That frightened them away from all intangible investments for quite some time.

As they continued to amass dollars, they tended to hold them and concentrate on getting maximum interest income. The huge excesses of dollars worried them, however, and they tried to switch them into German marks, Swiss francs, and Japanese yen. This dumping of dollars sent their value down, and further worsened the Arab plight for they were cheapening the very money that they had to go on accepting for their oil sales. They began to try buying real estate, but that absorbed only a small amount of what they had left over after importing all sorts of machinery and services from the West.

Gold from $250 to $800

So in late 1978, they began to buy gold more seriously than they had ever done before. That sent the price from $250 to over $800 in a matter of months. Amazingly, considering their reputation as traders, some Arabs were still major buyers near the $850 mark. Then they found out that when their own purchases were completed, few additional buyers were on hand to carry the market higher.

Where OPEC Money Is Now

That brings us to the present. You see now an Arab world that holds a very large part of the entire planet's wealth and continues to amass billions more every year, holding most of it in highly liquid form. The total amount of real estate and stocks—huge as they are—does not make up more than a small percentage of Arab assets.

They put quite a lot into their own neighbor nations and other parts of the developing world, although this is done unenthusiastically and only for public relations reasons. The Arab kingdoms and other conservative governments are being forever accused by their radical internal enemies of being Western puppets who have no interest in the welfare of their Arab brothers. So they make investments in the less-developed countries around them, with great fanfare, to prove this is not so.

But this is not where their heart or their wallet really is. *It is in U.S. Treasury bills and other notes, bonds, and similar obligations that pay substantial interest and can be moved at short notice.* This makes it "hot money." If too much of it is suddenly shifted, some currencies plummet, others soar, and interest rates go berserk.

But that also makes Arab money one of the most fascinating indicators for an investor to know about. This rising tide of liquidity cannot fail to search for new outlets; and wherever it goes, some market is going to be suddenly floated to great heights.

The Advice They Are Getting

Sometimes you can follow and step directly in the footprints of the Arabs in a very profitable way. This is especially true for short-term traders. In other cases—applicable to either traders or investors—it is more important to watch the effect they are having on a certain market and to be warned that the price may reverse after their buying stops. While there is no way, of course, to get exact information on just where the oil money will go next, there are ways to judge the most likely paths. First of all, those probable paths are few in number. Second, my familiarity with the general policies of the men who counsel the Arabs makes it possible to conclude which types of opportunities they will be more and more on the lookout for.

In chronological order, the Arabs are first being advised, as I write this, to keep the bulk of their funds in short-term interest-bearing loans while the rates are still high enough to give them adequate and easy profits. But the advisers sense that the very substantial fees they earn will require them to make a more creative contribution, especially as interest levels dip closer to the rate of inflation. For that means that the *real* earnings on the money will become very small, perhaps even a negative figure after taxes. The Arabs will then be forced to reinvest their money in other ways. And the four main moves that I foresee are these:

1. They will shift some cash into much longer-term loans.
2. They will buy two special types of U.S. real estate.
3. They will finally buy U.S. common stocks heavily.
4. They will begin buying far more commodities and futures contracts.

Arabs Look to the Longer Term

I know at first hand that Arab money is now actively searching for places where it can be safely invested at good rates of interest for ten to fifteen years or even longer. A good many American companies and banks are being quietly offered multimillion dollar loans—often up to a half-billion dollars— at rates 2 or 3% below the current market. The only stipulation is that they be well secured—signed by a major company and countersigned by an important U.S. bank, so that there is virtually no risk whatever.

Why would anyone be willing to lend cash at less than current market rates? Clearly, the Arab investors are expecting a long new cycle when interest rates come down and stay down for years. This does not mean that they are right, but it does tell us that more of their money will be put into such things as longer-term bonds, creating very sharp rallies at times.

Finally, I deduce from these current moves that many Arabs expect further political troubles with the West—serious enough to pose the threat that the United States and other governments might again block their assets here, as we did during the Iranian hostage crisis. That would seem to be the only reason for offering money at advantageous rates to private borrowers instead of buying long-term U.S. bonds that would give them a better return. The way they are setting up the present offerings seems designed to hide the Arab ownership in the background.

THE APPEAL OF WAREHOUSING

Warehouse facilities will draw some Arab investments and will consequently have one of the biggest moves in the real estate field. I find that the trend of construction costs is making it almost as expensive to build a warehouse as it is to build an equivalent-size office building. This, plus the growing need for such facilities, will make the rental return much closer to equal. Existing warehouses are presently priced at only about half the value of existing offices. The Arabs' financial advisers, and other alert analysts, will start to counsel investments in that kind of property. It will not be easy to firm up these decisions because the Arabs have been attracted mainly to prestige buildings. They like something that *looks* solid and impressive, and that produces provable, present income. To invest in a warehouse out near an airport or a railway siding—and one which is producing only a so-so present return at that—will not be appealing. But the desperate need to put cash somewhere will begin to overcome this reluctance. And as the first signs appear that these were indeed fine investments, there will be more of a rush into them.

What this means is that if you have some cash for real estate purposes and enough patience to wait a couple of years for signs of success, you can tap this same trend very profitably. It may require getting a few friends together to put up the necessary cash. Or you may find that a local realty firm is organizing a syndicate for the purpose, so that you can simply buy a share in the project. Study carefully, with these factors especially in mind:

- The location of the warehouse—convenience to incoming supplies and to eventual markets.
- The condition of the building—and how modern its facilities are for moving and storing goods efficiently.
- The price in relation to office buildings in the area—it should be very much lower per square foot.
- The financing—bear in mind that the less cash you have to put in, the greater the leverage.

Other than the above, and with the possible exception of very special buildings, such as professional centers or shopping malls in areas that have been notably deprived, I would be very cautious about any other kind of *constructed* real estate. Most of it has been sent to astronomical heights during the 1970's. Further increases should be at a much slower pace than the rise of other prices. But . . .

THE LURE OF FOOD

Farmland is the one other very special situation that will attract increasing amounts of Arab money. The world's need for food is going to put a rising premium on the unexpandable supply of land that is capable of growing it. The best information sources I know believe that the value of prime U.S. farmland will approximately triple in the next decade—helped along by dollars that we once sent to OPEC and that will be invested in our own rural properties.

Here again, the way of financing a purchase is all-important. If you can find a way to get reasonable loans and to carry them with income produced by the land itself, a big commitment to farmland can give a fine result. But remember that even with the best terms, this does depend on the uncertainties of each year's weather and crop prices.

Buying agricultural land requires knowledge and careful comparison of values. Anyone with enough time and interest can learn the facts and then gradually develop the judgment that leads to successful deals. But that kind of care is basic, and it is very dangerous to invest in any short-cut way.

BACK TO THE STOCK MARKET

When it comes to stocks, the Arabs will definitely come back in. Their old inclination to buy big blue chip shares will be moderated by the memory of what happened before. On the other hand, their more recent yen to buy hyperactive newer companies will be somewhat hampered by the fact that such firms have small capitalization—not much stock outstanding. Here and there, an Arab will form a joint venture with a young American entrepreneur. But when it comes to buying stock in an infant venture, the number of cases will be limited. This will leave as the chief alternative the medium-sized companies that I talk about in Chapter 9. And this is another reason why I stress such firms so much here. They are one of the great investment opportunities of our time, even without any Arab interest. *With* it, they will be propelled to much higher price-earning ratios.

It will at first seem to you that this is a much simpler, less bothersome way of investing your money than the real estate route mentioned above. In a way it is. You don't have to cruise in a car for hours on end, looking for properties, searching for partners or financing arrangements, or worrying about property conditions. But I do hope you will not regard stock buying as a quick way to invest with your left hand. It should be done with great attention to the condition of the company, the merit of its products, the soundness of its finances. As you will see, my notion of buying stocks is not very different from buying real property. They are not pieces of paper. They are pieces of companies—real estate included. And they *are* tangible investments. That's what the Arabs will come to recognize before long, and you can ride the uphill path with them.

TAKING POSITIONS IN COMMODITIES

Futures contracts will attract Arab investors too. Their advisers will point out to them that this need not be real gambling, but a form of canny trading, which has historically appealed to the Arab mind. When they do it, it will become less speculative because the new money will seek out only the situations that are fundamentally underpriced and with a plan to ride out the long trend. You will understand this better when you read the chapter on commodity trading. For now you should just be aware that this is another field into which some large amounts of cash are going to be injected. Remember the big, long moves that happened in the U.S. grain markets when the Soviets very shrewdly bought into them a few years ago.

In a sense, this principle of assessing what the very biggest investors are likely to do is a condensed and enriched form of what we do in any financial decision. There is always the question, even if unspoken, "What are other investors going to do?" Not because they are necessarily right, but because their cash will have an effect. If too many of them rush in, they will make the market overpriced and ultimately ruin it. At earlier stages, when the larger investors usually move in, they can bring a neighborhood, an industry, or a type of stock to life. Big fund managers are one major segment of these "other investors." The Arabs are a special group that has given us an even better chance of pinpointing our answers.

Whatever the field—farmland, warehouses, gold, or grains—the OPEC money will probably move in early. Such concentrated buying by a small group will send prices up explosively. But I want you to realize that this kind of buying can dry up rapidly. It usually encourages smaller investors to come in and bid prices even higher. But unless there is an overriding reason to believe in the long-run prospects, it is usually best to take substantial profits rather early in the move and not wait for the last dollar. The Arabs have a traditional trader's mentality, and they will usually try to sell quickly themselves. Their investments, in other words, will often be characterized by sharp run-ups and then sudden declines.

Reading What Money Managers Read

One simple thing you can do to keep abreast of "which way the big money is moving" is to read a monthly magazine called *The Institutional Investor.* It is primarily for money managers—all the way from the heads of major funds down to those who run rather modest trust departments of banks or pension funds of small companies. But anyone can subscribe to it or see it in some of the larger public libraries. You will find in it many indications of the varying directions being taken by the professional managers of all types. In this way, you can keep updating the points I have given above. My aim here is mainly to alert you to the *principle* of watching the big investors. As time goes on, they will adjust their directions, and you will want to do the same.

7

What You Should Know about the Stock Market

There is a great and continuing controversy over whether the stock market is smart or senseless. Of all the questions on which investment authorities hotly disagree, none looms quite as large. For if the market really points to the future, then knowing how to read its actions is a key to all planning—both for businessmen and for you as an investor. A falling market should warn companies to lighten their inventories, trim their payrolls, cut their expansion plans. An uptrend in stocks would spur them to spend and grow—creating more jobs, more customers. In other words, Wall Street's prophecies would be self-fulfilling.

I have a firm conviction that the market IS a remarkable crystal ball—each day's market makes part of a pattern that can confirm or adjust my forecast of what the economy and then the market itself is going to do in the next few years. I think, as many Wall Street professionals do, that stock prices always embody information that later proves to have been on target. This is true even when market action seems to clash with known facts about consumer spending, jobs, and corporate profits. The market knows best because it takes into account all these known facts plus a lot of unknown ones that are going to tip the balance.

And in that case, we have a prime way of verifying when the U.S. economy is shifting into each of the two stages that I have outlined for you.

The Best Barometer

Among the authorities who have traditionally deplored this idea are many government economists, for they become especially irritated when stock prices point opposite to their own optimistic assurances. "The market has foretold eight out of the last six recessions," goes the sarcastic comment that some of them like to make. They deride the notion that stocks give certain signals well in advance of a general business upturn and a different set of signs shortly before a slump.

"But any President's aides would do well to read the market action, rather than their own comments," says Michael Evans of Chase Econometrics Associates, a leading Wall Street research firm. "Of those six recessions since World War II, not one was predicted a year in advance by the President's Council of Economic Advisers."

Between the opposing views, my own definite conclusion is that the stock market—when properly interpreted—does come closer than any other barometer to forecasting the course of business. While not so infallible that you should invest your all on the sole basis of their signals, the indications can steer you toward opportunities and save you from costly mistakes.

Why, then, does this perceptive market jiggle so? Why do we read a 14-point rally one day and a sharp pullback a few days later? Says a leading broker who advises millionaire Europeans on when and how to invest in U.S. stocks: "On a day-to-day basis the market certainly has a genius for making no sense at all, but those rallies and dips are really very slight adjustments—only a few per cent of the total value. When you are driving a car at high speed, you keep moving the steering wheel in a series of jiggles. You jerk it even harder to avoid a bump. But all the while there is one main direction. It is like that with stocks. When seen over a period of time and matched against later developments, the market is almost perfect as an indicator."

Why the Market Knows

What makes it work that way? I believe the market knows more about people's true plans and convictions than any person or group can possibly learn. It's better than any poll or survey because it goes beyond merely asking people for a comment. Talking to a pollster costs nothing. But the vote cast by anyone who decides to buy or sell a share of stock means that he's backing his opinion with hard cash.

The composite that we call the market—totalling thousands of listed and unlisted stocks in giant corporations and fledgling local ventures—embodies all the confidence or fear, the aggressiveness or caution, the knowledge or doubt of millions of people. And included among them are businessmen with expert feel for the industries they are buying into or selling out of. It means they're looking beyond today and foreseeing certain conditions for the years to come.

Doubts about the market's ability to predict come from disagreement about two main points:

- The first is *which indicators to watch*.
- The second is *how far ahead they are pointing*.

I hope to simplify these enough to make them a practical tool for your use or, at the very least, a revealing background that helps you to grasp and assess the financial advice you get from brokers and publications.

Which Average to Follow

The professionals of Wall Street use many indicators beyond what the normal stock buyer works with. Aside from the Dow Jones Industrial Average, they check indexes of 65 stocks, 500 stocks, and the index of all New York Stock Exchange issues.

They watch chart patterns take shape from the trend of daily jiggles. They look for times when industrial stocks and the index of industrial production start moving upward together. They check the average level of transportation shares to see if this "confirms" what industrial stocks are showing. They wait for moments when the pessimism of the "odd-lotter" reaches its lowest point; this is the small investor who buys or sells in lots of less than 100 shares and who traditionally unloads his holdings at the bottom of the market, just when an upturn is near.

But there is reason to question whether so many measurements might not sometimes confuse the issue. Each one has provable merit; yet there are Wall Street specialists who feel that they get lost in the mass of details.

A Simple Approach

For the sake of simplifying and also because I believe it may be genuinely more effective, I want to suggest that you use just two main indicants in listening to "what the market is trying to tell you."

- The first is the plain old Dow Jones Average of 30 leading industrial stocks. Its role is sometimes derided because that number of companies seems such a narrow basis for judging the economy. When just a few of those 30 firms have problems, the DJIA can look very sick, as it did in 1977 when U.S. Steel, Bethlehem Steel, Eastman Kodak, and DuPont all encountered bad news. These four issues pulled down the Dow Jones while other measuring rods—such as Standard & Poor's 500-stock average—were doing much better and the average of over-the-counter stocks actually was rising. But just as the first half-hour of election night returns on TV so often reflects the main outcome, it is remarkable how often the Dow Jones Average turns out to signal the basic path that will eventually be confirmed by the other indicators. Even if only four companies first pulled the average down in 1977, the fact that steel, photography, and chemicals were all ailing at once did prove to be sign of wider woes to come.

- The other indicant you can use easily is the bond market. There is a delicate balance between the current return on bonds and dividends from stock. Money managers constantly compare these before deciding where to put their cash. You need not trouble with all the fine points that go into the comparison. It is enough to know that when fixed-income securities are paying high rates (in other words, when bond prices are *down*), the people who control big money find less reason to take risks in stocks. And whether they are right or wrong, their avoidance of big stock investment will weigh the market down.

All through the sluggish period of the mid-1970's, for instance, Charles E. Woodman, Vice President of Smith, Barney, Harris Upham & Co., kept saying, "There's nothing much 'wrong' with the stock market. It's just that bonds look more attractive. Investors will keep pulling in those cash returns until stocks become irresistible bargains." Finally, though, Woodman detected that such a time had come. "Many companies are now using cash to buy their own shares," he noted. "That's a sign they consider it the most profitable way to put the money to work. And many firms are bidding to take over other companies. In other words, they find it cheaper to buy an existing business through the stock market than to build new facilities of their own. That means stocks are becoming a cheap way of buying good value." Within months a 200-point rally was under way.

Both measuring gauges that I suggest to you are easy ones for anyone to follow. Even small-town newspapers carry the Dow Jones Industrial Average and brief reports on the activity in the bond market.

What to Watch For

What are you looking for the DJIA to do? Is it simply to go up or down? No. The averages rise and fall so often that it takes more than that to give a real picture. It takes a pattern. When

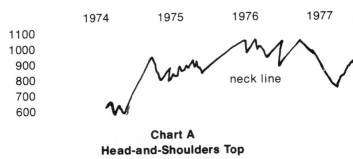

Chart A
Head-and-Shoulders Top
(signaling a probable fall)

the average moves narrowly for a few months, then advances to a new high point, then falls back and moves in a small range again, as in Chart A, that is called a head-and-shoulders top. It is very often a signal of a major decline. When that whole picture is inverted, as in Chart B, it is a head-and-shoulders bottom formation. And that very often foretells a major advance. Most newspapers with financial pages carry such charts that reflect market action. So does *Barron's,* the financial weekly. You can find these in public libraries.

The bond market activity is even easier to follow. The small jiggles in rates can be ignored. Just watch for those days when

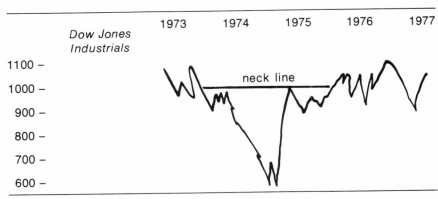

Chart B
Head-and-Shoulders Bottom
(signaling a probable rise)

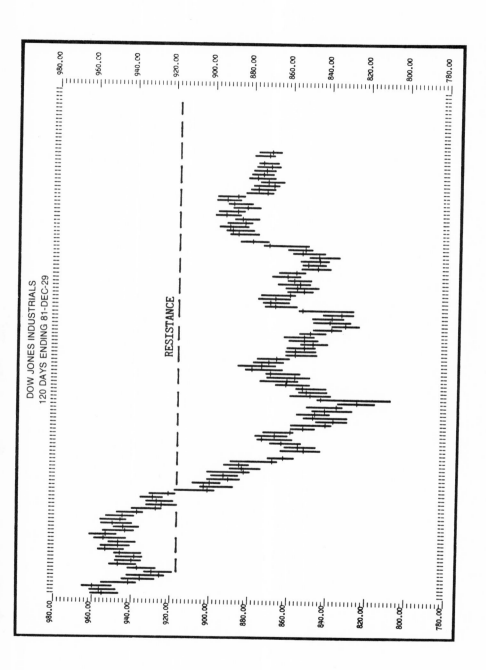

DOW JONES INDUSTRIALS
120 DAYS ENDING 81-DEC-29

RESISTANCE

it is said either that the bond market dropped sharply—which will be bad news for stocks before long—or that it climbed steeply. In the latter case, there is a good chance that it is signaling future stock advances. Watch it daily for a long enough period of time to recognize that the path it is on is really a trend. Three consecutive weeks when bonds are higher at the close than they were the previous Friday is a reasonable indication of an uptrend. If they are lower on three successive Fridays, the chances are strong that this is a real downtrend.

The Question of Time

Let me explain that in order to be a crystal ball, the stock market often has to ignore today's situation. It may be going down at a time when business is still looking pretty good. Economic indicators then take a few months to start revealing the trouble, after which company reports show a decline for a year or longer. By the time the trough of this fall is reached, stocks have been tumbling for perhaps 18 to 24 months. By then they're again looking ahead to the eventual rebound in business. So stocks are steady or starting to climb just when everyone looking around sees high unemployment, poor sales, disappointing company earnings. This leads even some very knowledgeable professionals to say—wrongly—that "the market isn't making sense."

Take the toboggan slide that started in January, 1973 when business was still apparently healthy. The fall was attributed to Watergate uncertainties at the time, but looking back, it's apparent that nothing really upsets stocks for long except the prospect of lower profits. Business didn't drop off enough to prove the market right until mid-1974. The D-J industrials kept falling, reached the low point of 577.60, then began to recover while business was still in terrible shape.

"Unemployment soared," says Louis Engle, a well-known Wall Street analyst and market author. "Dividends were cut or passed entirely; various leading economic indicators just dropped, dropped, dropped. It wasn't until the stock market

Chart C

How Far Ahead the Stock Market Anticipated Turns in Business Activity
(This is approximate, as there have been changes in the types of averages used)

	Failed to Anticipate	1–2 mos.	3–6 mos.	6–8 mos.	9–12 mos.
Business peaks (prior to a fall)	1899, 1929	1890,1909, 1919,1923, 1937,1957	1886,1895 1902,1907 1912,1948 1960	1953	1892,1968 1973
Business low points (prior to an upturn)		1914	1890,1938 1949,1960 1974	1900 1903 1907 1932 1957 1970	1888 1893 1896 1910 1923 1953

had recovered more than 40 per cent in the spring of 1975 that business first showed indications of being ready to turn upward . . ."

That understanding of the link between today's prices and the long-term prospects is basic. As *The Wall Street Journal* once put it, the market "measures cumulative profits of all companies so far into the future one might as well say the horizon is infinite."

So to make sense out of stock market behavior, you have to discard the idea that it has anything much to do with today's news. You have to expect an average wait of several months between the time you notice a stock market signal and the actual start of a new economic cycle.

As Chart C shows, the market has anticipated major turning points in business 35 times in the past century and failed to anticipate only twice. In the hectic world of finance, that adds up to a remarkable record. Most of the signals that the market had peaked and was about to turn downward gave rather short warnings, as you will see—around one to six months. Indications of an upturn tended to be longer in advance—more often 6 to 12 months.

Reacting to Signals

The final question that you want to zero in on, of course, is specifically what to do when these signals are noticed. Take this situation: Say the Dow Jones Average hit a new low two months ago after six months of drifting sidewise. It has since moved up a little and is trading unexcitingly around the levels where it was just before that last plunge. This is a strong indication that a business upturn is some months ahead and that the market may begin a sharp upward move very soon. Start to study the behavior of stocks you like, getting the latest data on company performance to be sure they are still your choices. Meanwhile, watch the bond market each day as well. If there is an abrupt rise in bond prices—"a drop in yields," as the papers often headline it—this tends to confirm what the stock market has been saying.

You may not feel confident enough of your interpretation to use these signals as a command to go and buy stocks. Perhaps you will want to read what financial journals are saying, talk to an experienced broker, and so on. But at least you will have a view of your own to compare with what others advise, and even to question their opinions. The trend in recent years has been for small investors to perform unusually well, and sometimes to outdo the professionals. Even those odd-lot statistics I mentioned earlier tend to become cloudy these days, because the people who buy and sell in small quantities occasionally seem to react better than the fund managers who are burdened with blocks of stock that freeze them into over-caution. So don't underrate your ability to feel the market's pulse. It may play a big part in the investment decisions coming up.

Charts: "A Picture of What People Are Doing"

Among those Wall Street observers who feel that the market's past action points to the future, none go quite as far in that conviction as that special fraternity of market analysts known as "chartists," or "technicians." Some of these analysts insist that a chart that shows the ups and downs of any one stock, or of the whole market, embodies every factor, known or unknown, that will affect the future. According to this view, it is unimportant to be familiar with the fundamental facts. A correct reading of the chart tells it all.

Most technicians, however, are less dogmatic. Along with them, I believe that the chart pinpoints most of the favorable possibilities and, more important, shows most of the danger signs. I see it as the background picture against which other facts can be interpreted.

Lawrence H. Heim is typical of this approach, and his location in Portland, Oregon also underscores how nationwide is the great market we still call Wall Street. "I never think of my charts as having any magical qualities," says Heim. "I look at them as a picture of what people are doing. The main trend lines and the intermediate wiggles tell me that people reacted in certain ways over and over again in the past—bought heavily at some point, hung on grimly at other times, sold hastily here and there. So when I see that same pattern forming again, I instinctively think, 'People don't change much. They'll probably react that way again at this point and this one.'" When risks look high to Heim, he may tell investors to stay on the sidelines altogether for months at a time—to keep their money 100% in cash wherever it earns good interest.

But suppose there's a conflict between good news making the rounds about a company and a warning signal on Heim's charts? "I usually tell clients to stay away from that stock," says Heim. "Not because I am sure the chart is right and the news is wrong. But because the technical warning means that the odds against me are greater in that stock. Why take the greater risk?

"The knack of making money is to find profit opportunities while holding losses as low as possible. The charts help me to find situations where the odds are best."

Charts like these are the technician's tea leaves. In Chart B, Heim shows the "classic and massive head-and-shoulders bottom formation" that developed around the 1974 stock market low point. The DJIA rose dramatically after breaking the neckline. Says Heim: "An astute investor who had learned to recognize certain important chart formations could have predicted the stock market rise that started in late 1975, and he would have made his stock purchase at or prior to the point where the neckline was broken."

8

Quick In-and-Out Trading of Stocks

It is common to refer to speculators unfavorably as though they were somewhat reprehensible. I consider that a badly uninformed attitude. Without short-term traders there would be no stock market. They are the ones who are always there, prepared to buy any kind of stock if the price seems right, and, therefore, make the exchanges into a true market. You might say that they keep the store open, so that the long-term investor is always assured of a place to buy or sell whenever he feels the need of it.

One thing more: The firmly implanted notion that trading is more dangerous is wrong. The investor who gets caught in a long market slide may see a very large part of his holdings eaten away. If he holds on to good stocks long enough, they will recover. But all too often, the average investor sells at a low point and then stays out until the market is high again. The good trader is never caught in such a snare. As soon as the turndown is apparent, he is dealing in the opposite direction—selling stocks short and making whatever gains he can on the downside. Or he may buy for quick gains on brief rallies. Even when his moves go wrong, he gets out with small losses, rather than allowing himself to be trapped for long.

Which of the two makes the most money? My own experience indicates that, on the average, it is the patient investor. Among other things, it takes less skills to select a few good situations and stay with them than to assess the whole market and a new set of companies on a day-to-day basis. There are a good many persons who have the judgment and the patience to let one or two good stocks build up to a major holding over the years. I have known only a very few traders—even the professionals—who manage to be right often enough to equal those gains. But the task of making wise long-term commitments will become harder as we go into the turbulent second half of the 1980's.

So you may find it valuable to know some basic facts about short-term trading. Because even when you buy a stock with the intention of holding it for a while, you want to buy it as cheaply as possible; and when you finally decide to sell you want to get the best price. The trader's ways serve you in very good stead for those purposes. So I will touch on some of the main things to watch for in trying to decide which way a stock or the entire market is about to move.

Power of the Unknown

The single greatest thing to keep in mind in short-term trading is that stocks move on unknown factors—for hidden reasons. Once a fact has been announced, the reason to act on it is already largely gone. Because this is so, the most important sign you can get is an unexplainable move. If either a single stock or the entire market starts to climb for no visible reason, this is the most bullish signal you will ever get. If you are a potential buyer, it is time to *buy*. Don't wait to learn the explanation; by that time, you will have been joined by many other buyers at a far higher price level. If you had been thinking of selling, *wait* a bit, because you will get a better price before long.

The same thing applies to an unexplained decline. It is the most bearish—most unfavorable signal of all. Don't optimistically assume that perhaps it means nothing, that since all the visible signs are fine the stock will probably recover nicely. Whenever a stock or a market moves without apparent reason, *there IS a reason*. Some people who know more than the general public are starting to act on it. Anyone who moves fast to act in that same way has an above-average chance of profiting.

Signal to Sell

Take the example of a company which I have followed carefully and whose stock had been doing well for some months. Bergen Brunswig Corp., back in the late 1970's, is a good case in point. This distributor of wholesale drug products had climbed from $7 or $8 a share to $18, largely on publicity and good reports of a new venture in the medical insurance field. Suddenly, it staggered. Occasional drops of ½ or ¾ point are routine after such a rise. But this one fell 2½ points one day, recovered a trifle, then dropped another 1¾. All rumors of trouble were denied. People who considered themselves insiders insisted that this was just profit taking and that nothing could be wrong.

But bit by bit, the story came out: Errors in calculation had caused big losses in this new medical insurance venture, and large additional claims might multiply these losses disastrously. As fact piled upon fact, the stock kept falling. At one point it got as low as 4½—far too low because the fundamentally sound and well-run firm had already shored up its position by then. It rose to over $30 a share later on, although it took over three years.

As seen with a trader's mentality, anyone who owned Bergen Brunswig when it took that first sharp drop from $18 should have sold it, either then, or certainly at the time of its second sharp drop. The fact that it was down to $14 by then should not have deterred him. For even if he was determined to stay with that firm's stock for years, he could have bought three times as much of it later on with the proceeds of that $14 sale.

Moves to Watch For

The overall stock market, although subject to more variable factors, can sometimes give a strong buy or sell signal in a similar way. If a lagging market in a dull economic time moves up by a few points, there is no significance in it at all. But if there is a 20-point rise out of the blue at a time like that, the chances are that more gains will follow in the weeks ahead.

Here again, there IS a reason. Perhaps there have been many short sellers in the market, all convinced that it is going to drift lower. When it starts to climb on this particular day, it hits certain levels that make them decide to liquidate those short positions—which involves buying stock to cover what they had sold short. So the newspapers will say that it was "just a technical rally, triggered by short covering." But the deeper fact is that there *were* many short sellers in the market and that prices were so near the threshhold which would induce them to turn around and buy. It means that the invisible valley where downhill action suddenly turns uphill had been reached. If this 20-point day had occurred after a presidential speech or a Federal Reserve Board change in interest-rate policy, it would be only mildly interesting. It is the unknown cause that gives it power.

So let me repeat for emphasis a rule that is so simple yet can mean so many dollars to you over the years: *Nothing is so meaningful as a stock move that has no apparent cause.* As the real reason becomes gradually known to a broadening number of people, it will create more and more of a move in that same direction.

By no "apparent cause" I do not mean the pat little phrases that are used by news writers to explain the previous day's action. "Short covering," "profit taking," "triggering stop-loss orders," and so on. These are symptoms, not causes. A genuine cause must be a new cloud or a new ray of sunlight appearing on the economic horizon.

For example, if a group of corporate earnings reports come out with far better profits than anyone expected, it is no surprise to see the market rise—and not very significant either. The news is out; the market result has already occurred. And that's that. If there is a sudden ominous drop in the value of the U.S. dollar on exchange markets, a stock market decline is expectable and, therefore, has no predictive value. But if nothing basic happens—no big change in the unemployment figure, no huge jump in inflation, in interest rates, or in the nation's money supply figures, no sudden veer in the leading indicators, in auto sales, in construction, or in retail sales— then a large move in stocks has a hidden meaning.

The Market versus The News

This is all the more true if something dramatic happens and the market moves *opposite* to what would be expected. Such was the case in October, 1981 when President Sadat of Egypt was assassinated. By bringing the danger of a Mideast war and an oil-supply crisis much closer, this event was widely expected to cause a massive stock market drop. But after staggering briefly, stocks actually started to rise. Short-term traders knew it had to mean that some offsetting good news was on the way. If they bought without waiting to find out what it might be, they benefited from a quick 40-point gain. It was clear later that this was because important reductions in the prime rate had been shaping up. They began to be made in the following days.

Although such moves may be short-lived, you can see how even a steady investor can benefit. Hundreds of stocks were 8% to 12% higher than they had been a few days earlier. Anyone who had planned, for whatever reason, to sell a long-term holding and who held off briefly because the market didn't agree with the front-page news got a much better price for his shares.

How Cash Fuels Stocks

A second point for you to absorb and make a part of your financial thinking is that the stock market is like a see-saw with a large pile of common stocks on one side and a big supply of cash on the other. The number of stocks seldom changes much. It is only when a lot more money is heaped on to one side that the stocks are forced upward. But when money is suddenly taken away to be used elsewhere, the stocks fall sharply.

What can cause cash to be moved away from the stock market in this fashion? It is competition from other markets. Only if some alternative form of investment looks more attractive than stocks will the managers of major mutual funds, pension funds, and other billion-dollar institutions put their cash elsewhere. And it is the level of interest rates, more than any other single factor, that can lead them to this decision. When they can get only 7% or 8% return on their money in bonds, Treasury bills, or money market funds, they are usually inclined to keep a considerable portion of their cash in stocks because they are well paid as experts and they don't like admitting that all they can do is park the cash in an interest-bearing account just like everyone else. But when interest rates go up into the teens, the pull of that sure gain is too great to be ignored. And so they do keep the money working in that way until and unless the outlook for corporate profits becomes overwhelming.

The Money Supply

This is why there is so much anxious watching of the Federal Reserve Board's policy on interest rates, and of the weekly money supply figures. If the money supply seems to be growing too rapidly (thereby threatening to worsen inflation) the Federal Reserve Board is more likely to tighten credit; and any move to make money less plentiful is sure to result in higher interest rates.

If you are an *investor* and interested in the day-to-day market only as a matter of general background, these interest rates and money supply figures will serve to give you a sense of direction. In the case that you have some of your cash in short-term trading, statistics of this kind are more crucial.

Get to know the days when these figures are released by the government. Try to avoid trading on those days because a surprise figure—almost always released after the market's close—can make your price look very poor on the following morning. Pay close attention, too, to the action of the bond markets, which is reported on the ticker that comes into your broker's office. They are much more immediately sensitive to interest rates than the stock market, so you may get a clue that you can instantly translate into a stock decision—before other stock traders get the same notion.

Say, for example, that a relatively quiet bond market suddenly drops sharply one afternoon. This means bond *prices* are lower, but making bond *yields* greater. It points to higher interest rates. The bond market could be wrong, of course, but a sharp movement there is seldom without some foundation. So it is wise to assume that interest rates will be moving upward for a time, thereby draining cash away from stocks. It points to a downward push for stocks in the short run. If you have a stock that you were thinking of selling anyway, do it at once, before the general market falls and, perhaps, robs you of another point or two.

Three Vital Signs

When it comes to timing the action of a specific stock, there are three main signs to look for:

- If the price begins to rise on expanding volume, it is an indication that important money is starting to bet on the stock. If you have researched the company and like its prospects, this kind of action is a signal to buy promptly.
- If there is a rumor of good news—such as a merger or a stock split—you may get a chance for a very short-term profit. The key rule to remember in this case is: "Buy on the rumor; sell on the fact." As soon as the rumor is confirmed, traders will sell out, because there is no longer any mystery to spur a further quick advance. But if you do take an interest in acting on a rumor, be sure the action of the stock is also favorable—rising on expanding volume. It's the only indication that the rumor is not a flimsy concoction which will be ignored by others.

- If a company's fortunes take a major turn, you have a great opportunity. Nothing is more lucrative than to spot a turnaround situation. A good many corporate happenings can greatly affect a stock: Introduction of a promising new product is one. Taking over another company usually spurs the price. Or being taken over by a large firm can be even more of a stimulus. On the unfavorable side, a sudden government suit, a recall of its products because of defects, or announcement of big inroads into its market by a competitor are among the factors that can cause a sharp drop. But most of these things are known to the public before you can act on them. The trader's chance to benefit comes when the well-known news fades from public attention and a new trend quietly takes over.

Let's stay with the same company whose unfavorable example I gave earlier in this chapter. There was Bergen Brunswig with a black eye resulting from its one terrible venture into a new field. So, many speculators who had bid its stock up too high kept selling out and pushing its price down to ridiculously low levels. No one thought of it as anything but a bad-news situation. Well, some company reverses of that kind do prove to be fatal. There is no law that says a depressed stock must come back. But it is worth watching because a competent management can sometimes make a complete U-turn.

The Bergen Brunswig people kept their heads, worked hard on the lines they knew, settled the old claims, and took all their losses in one terrible year; they began to build their earnings higher, quarter after quarter. Hardly anyone noticed. The stock did move up from 4¼ to 6. Then 6¾. Up to 9 and back to 8. And so on. But anyone following it, reading its quarterly reports, would have noticed the steady improvement of its figures, the sound cash management, the higher return on capital, and the elimination of debt. A classic turnaround situation. The stock suddenly spurted into the teens, the twenties, and up to 35 before it paused.

Betting Against First Reactions

Of the innumerable pointers one could give for short-term stock movements, just one more is absolutely essential for you to know: *The public's first reaction to spot news is always wrong.*

Say there is a sudden war scare. A report that the Soviets are staging troop maneuvers near an East European country, and the fear that the United States might get involved. The stock market promptly falls 15 or 20 points. Why? Because so many persons instantly call their brokers and sell stocks. Not only amateurs. Even some sophisticated traders do it, not because they think stocks should fall, but because they know that it *will* happen for a matter of hours and they want to make a quick profit.

Meanwhile, no one at all jumps in to buy—no one, that is, except the "specialists" who have a responsibility under exchange rules to keep the trading as steady as possible. They do their duty by absorbing any stock that is being dumped in this helter-skelter fashion. But their duty is also highly profitable. By the next morning or very soon after it, thousands of persons have had time to reflect that there probably will be no war, that the United States and NATO will only add to their defense readiness, and that, in any case, hostilities are likely to be bullish for many stocks in the end.

Why, then, did the market go down in the first place? Because the uncertainty of a confused situation kept all buyers out and made some people panic enough to sell without knowing quite why. They just wanted to be out of everything.

What does that tell you about a practical use you could put this principle to? Any time there is a sudden sell-off on frightening news, you can jump in and move opposite to the direction of the market. You will be correct more than nine times out of ten. The market will move right back to where it was within a day or two. Nothing as big as a war scare has to happen. The report of a presidential illness will do it. Or the news that some country is breaking relations with us, is recalling its ambassador, or is threatening to pull out of the NATO alliance.

The public's first frightened reaction is wrong because stocks are not really much affected by a president's health or an international incident. Stocks depend mainly on hard financial facts. Most happenings that make headlines don't do much for or against profits. In the long run, one president's effects are much like another's, since the whole government is involved, the Congress and all. Slowly, in the course of many months or more likely years, a government can change the profitability of companies and therefore the proper level of stock prices. But not in a day.

The market's response to a big news break should usually be none at all. If you go in opposite to the market's movement, you will at least get the benefit of the corrective action. In the cases where a war really does develop, many companies can actually benefit from the opportunities it brings with it. Why should anyone want to *sell* aircraft and weapons companies if there is going to be a war? Lots of people do just that—for a few hours. The quick trader who goes in and buys as those stocks dip can turn a fast profit. But more important to the majority of patient investors are these twin facts:

- If you have buying in your mind, use a time like that to do it. It is a bargain opportunity.
- If you are frightened into the thought of selling, don't. Even if other factors make you want to sell a certain stock, be sure to avoid it during a time of confusing spot news. Wait a few days, and you will get a better price.

9

Buying Shares in Companies

I said earlier that the difference between a short-term speculator and a long-term investor is partly a matter of *time*. But
it is more than that. Another important distinction is *attitude*. The speculator is looking for situations in which others
are wrong, hoping to buy what most persons have overlooked or to sell before they think of bailing out. The investor
hopes that the value of his own assets will expand because the
general consensus favors them.

The part of you that is a patient investor—remember that
you can have parts of your money and your enthusiasm in two
arenas at once—sincerely hopes that other persons in the market will be successful and efficient. In this case, you are looking for companies that will go on growing as they have grown
before, for managements that will live up to their earlier
promise, and for a group ride with other stockholders who
all move along with the growth of this particular company.

Note the word *company*. Although you buy shares of stock,
I urge you to think of yourself as becoming a partner in a
business. If a local businessman approached you and suggested that you put some money into his new venture, what
points would you look for? His background and character, the
financial soundness of his plan, and the quality of his product
or service. In short, whether you like the looks of his business.

If you pick stocks that way, you will be right four times out of five.

Where to Study

The best way to make a start is by going into the research library of any well-staffed brokerage office to study their literature. You will always be made welcome because they know that your personal research is the first step toward orders that produce commissions. You will find any number of compilations of stocks that show which ones have had steady earnings growth for ten years running, which ones have paid increased dividends for a certain number of years, which are selling below book value, and so on.

In a matter of hours, you will begin to spot names of companies that seem to have a place on most of these favorable lists. You can then look up those companies, one by one, in a directory called *Standard & Poor's* that has a loose-leaf page or two of factual data for each of the thousands of companies listed on the New York or American Exchanges, or sold over the counter.

Then comes the big step that makes this *your personal investment* and not just a mechanical reaction to what some outside adviser suggests: Really think about what each of these firms makes—the concept that gives it a reason for existence. Is it filling a need that seems likely to last or to grow? Is it making something unique, or something better than others offer? Does the record show that others with more expert knowledge than yours seem to have been attracted to this company over the years? And if it makes a consumer product or renders a service to consumers, is it something that you personally have tried and like?

That last simple point can be very significant. It is amazing how often a one-man opinion poll proves to foretell how millions of others would vote too. If a new item appears on retail counters that adds to your personal comfort or pleasure, the chances are good that your fellow citizens will also like it and make the cash registers ring. Conversely, if you try something and don't like it, be a little wary of that company's stock, even if the statistics still show no sign of trouble.

Spotting Winners Early

Why go to all the effort of searching through literature, rather than heeding the stories on business pages or the suggestions of brokers about which stocks look exciting? Mainly because the purest gems are usually lying unseen. By the time a company is widely written about, its stock has probably risen a long way due to the buying of insiders, financial analysts, brokers, and other eager investors. It may still have a long way to go—so I do not at all mean that you brush off every suggestion from a knowledgeable and reputable financial man—but the price you pay is already rewarding many others who got there ahead of you. The greater satisfaction and the far greater profit comes from spotting a few firms that have not yet become popular or that have been dormant for a while.

The General Climate

Now before you move in to become a shareholder in the companies you like, you must take a broad look at what you think the overall market is going to do in the next few months. As you know, I expect the market to show great strength for the next couple of years. But any period includes enough ups and downs to make a considerable difference in how much stock costs you. Look at any list of shares, large and small, solid or speculative, and you will find that nearly all of them tended to be affected whenever the Dow Jones Average fell back. This is partly psychological, true; but there are some real and sensible factors in it.

I explained earlier why it is wrong to believe that "the market is crazy" and that its behavior is purely emotional. There is a lot of simple arithmetic behind what often appears capricious. For example, a falling market suddenly shrinks the holdings of millions of persons and many institutions. Instead of seeing their equity expand and gain more buying power, they see it contract. Many of them get margin calls and they are forced to sell something in order to put up more cash. They first sell stocks that appeal to them least; but if the fall continues, they have to sell even the most desirable ones. Meanwhile, people who would like to be buying at those prices are also crimped for cash. More sellers and fewer buyers—that equals lower prices for just about all stocks.

I already covered, in the preceding chapter, some of the ways to estimate whether the market looks strong or weak for the coming months. Since I am talking here about long-term investment, you don't have to pinpoint your timing to the exact start of a rising trend. Some historic investment buying opportunities come even earlier, as others grow more discouraged, dump their stocks, and preferably when they conclude that the market may never rise again. For soon after that, there will be few sellers left. Almost everyone will have fled, and anyone with cash can scoop up the spoils at really rockbottom prices. It is every investor's dream to move in at just such a point. But even apart from the moment of major reversal, it is possible to foretell most of the market's important moves. In the next chapter I will give you a set of rules for making sense of what seems to be haphazard ups and downs.

Once your use of these guidelines assures you that this is not the start of a bear market, that the overall environment is anywhere from neutral to bullish, you will want to know how to select and buy the specific companies that seem the most likely to go a long way.

The Growing Industries

The next step begins with a look at whole *groups* of companies, lines of business that are basically more expansive than most . . . or safer than most. Stocks of industries with uncommon growth prospects have a far better chance of rewarding your investment handsomely.

Your own observations and your study of brokerage research literature will give you ideas of which lines these are.

But some of your findings need to be looked at with a cynical eye because a history of past growth—even if it is the recent past—does not prove that this pace will continue. Take oilfield machinery, for example. Most analysts insist that this will continue to shine in the future, just as it has been doing for most of the past decade. That is because they foresee an insatiable world demand for more oil which will lead to un-ending exploration. But, as I said at the outset, I believe that excess supplies of oil will be the rule for more years than not in the coming decade. So I doubt that the very high growth rates of past years will continue in the companies that make oilfield equipment. I am similarly skeptical that the fast food industry will keep growing at the 15% to 20% rate of recent years, or that airlines will regain their old pace of 13% or 14% yearly expansion.

In the unusual two-stage time ahead of us, the selection of long-term holdings has to be narrowed to industries that are likely to take bad business conditions in stride and that also have high growth potential. These include:

- Computers
- Cable television
- Broadcasting
- Medical products and services
- Hospital equipment
- Electronics
- Property and casualty insurance
- Publishing
- Precision instruments
- Soft drinks
- Trucking

Also worthy of inclusion are companies that control totally new technology, such as computer-assisted design and bio-engineering. And firms with highly specialized military hardware are often beyond the reach of market ups and downs—makers of fighter-plane ejection seats, fire-control devices for tanks, laser-beam weaponry, and so on.

Examples of firms within some of these industries that are unusually strong financially and that have advantages in bucking hard times include: American Home Products, American Telephone & Telegraph, Carnation Company, Continental Corp., Johnson & Johnson, Kellogg, Texas Utilities, and Rochester Telephone. But these are cited just as *examples*. For the reason given before, your greatest gains will come from uncovering companies that have not been publicized recently. And the selection of those specific firms is the next step in the process.

Selecting Companies

There are at least four rules that I want you to keep firmly in mind. These are followed by some of the wisest financial managers for deciding which of the companies they basically like also have the statistical foundations to back up their optimism:

1. *The stock is selling below book value.* In other words, when the net assets—all the assets minus all the liabilities— divided by the number of shares outstanding give a figure higher than the stock's market price. The only trouble with this highly respected rule is that some of a company's long-term assets often have a questionable or controversial value and might not really be worth all that much if they had to be sold in a pinch. So I suggest a more refined and sophisticated approach, which is to calculate the short-term assets—cash, inventories, and accounts receivable—and then subtract the firm's total liabilities to get the net quick assets. This is *much* easier to do than it sounds. The descriptive sheet on each company that your stockbroker provides will show a statement of condition that is boiled down to just eight or ten rounded numbers. If this figure divided by the number of outstanding shares still gives a figure higher than the price of the stock, it's a very positive indication.

Now bear in mind that a company has to have a thriving business to make its stock go places. So just having a lot of cash and other quick assets won't ensure that its stock will do anything but dawdle. If, however, you have a company with plans and products that look good to you, the fact that its stock is priced below what the assets could bring in a forced sale means that you are paying absolutely nothing for the business itself—for the profit-making organization that is working for each shareholder. The stock may keep being overlooked for a while, but when it does get noticed, the gains will be big ones.

2. *The company's capitalization is small.* Just take the present selling price of the stock and multiply it by the total number of shares outstanding. When you do that for GE, IBM, DuPont, and so on, you get a figure in the billions. It will take that many more billions of new dollars invested in it to make the stock double. In most cases, a gain of 15 or 20% is about as big a jump as you can hope for. But if a firm has just one million shares outstanding, and they are selling at $15 a share, the financial world is valuing the whole company and its future prospects at only $15,000,000. It will take only $15,000,000 more—a petty cash figure in Wall Street—to double the stock's price. So a piece of good news about a blue chip company may add only a few percent to the value of a share, while a similar report about a smaller firm will add 50%.

If that sounds as if I am talking about quick speculation again, let me put it another way. A well-chosen firm with small capitalization can gain five or ten times as much for you in the next five years as a similar investment in a giant company can yield.

3. *The ratio of price to earnings is low.* I think this commonest of all stock-buying rules is somewhat overrated, but it should not be ignored. What's wrong with it is the assumption that a low P/E ratio—say, one that prices the stock at only six times the yearly earnings—guarantees its moving up to a more normal ratio of 12 or 14 times earnings. Not so at all. Just as some houses in a sleepy neighborhood may be cheap and stay cheap, some stocks that fail to excite investors with their prospects may stay at a very low P/E ratio.

BUT . . . if your brokerage firm or your own reading of business magazines and financial pages alerts you to a stock that has at other times been attractive to the investment community, that has enjoyed high P/E figures and then tumbled in that statistic because of temporary misfortunes, you have an interesting situation. Bear in mind that the price-to-earnings figure is an emotional one—a common assessment of where the earnings *will be going,* rather than where they are now. So if your other research leads you to conclude that the company profits are due to rebound, you may benefit from a double dose of tonic. If the profits rise by say $1 per share, that would add $5 to the stock's price even at the present P/E level. But the fact that earnings seem to be improving will probably raise the P/E ratio to 7, 10, or 12 to 1, so that $1 in higher earnings may make a $12 difference in the stock price.

4. *The stock fell abnormally in the last bear market.* Take note that I am not talking of any drop recorded in a recent decline lasting weeks or months, but of a bear market movement that persisted for at least a year and perhaps several years. Whenever your overall market view leads you to believe that the decline is about over and a long surge is ahead, take a careful look at how the stocks you like performed during that whole downward period. Check where they were at the start and how much they came down over the entire time. Now the conventional wisdom is to buy stocks that performed best—that fell least—during such a downtrend. *Not so.* That is a way to tie yourself to the slow movers and limit your future gains.

The stocks that fell most are the ones to favor now. Here and there, a huge decline may point to a permanently sick company, but your careful study will spot any such situation. Once that is eliminated, the other heavy losers will generally outperform the ones that seemed to do better on the downward leg. The reason is rather simple and straightforward: Any free market swings in pendulum fashion. It goes too far to the upside, then falls farther than it should. This is not only true of the market as a whole, but also of each individual stock. This principle is most vigorously at work on the ones that fall most. You might say that they have a more active pendulum; Wall Street language usually calls them "more volatile." Either way, they are the stocks likeliest to move upward strongly to the great joy of their shareholders. And considering that they start the next phase from a position of being unusually undervalued, they have quite a lot more room for gain.

This is not a theory; it is a documented fact. The stocks that fell most in recent bear markets usually outperformed the market average by a good 50% in the ensuing bull market. And *that* is a lot of dollars for the people who bought them.

Low Price, High Gain

Simple as those four rules are to understand and follow, there is one of my own that has a childlike simplicity: It is to concentrate most of your market investment dollars in stocks that sell for less than $20 a share. This doesn't mean to throw away all the other guidelines. You need them because there are thousands of stocks to choose from in the under-$20 category. The preceding rules will help you to decide which of them you should pay the most attention to. But by turning away from the costlier issues—even though some of them may do extremely well for their backers—you shift into a sort of overdrive gear where the leverage is enormously greater.

I am not talking of flimsy businesses, by any means. Many of these under-$20 stocks have annual sales of $200 million and above, have been consistently profitable for years, and have all the qualifications noted earlier in this chapter: They will fall little more or no more than the most renowned blue chip when the going gets rough. But when the move is upward, they have far more thrusting power. In a recent upward market move, while the Dow Jones Industrials were climbing 30%, a randomly selected group of stocks also listed on the N.Y. Stock Exchange but priced under $20 rose by more than 200%.

Again, I have to emphasize: Too many investors have been brainwashed into believing in a looking-glass world where true and false are reversed. What has been called conservatism has really been bad gambling technique. If at the race track things were arranged so that tickets paying off at 10 to 1 won just as often as the ones paying off at 5 to 4, only the mad and the foolish would bet on favorites. As it is, betting on favorite horses can make sense because they win more often. Favorite stocks don't. Betting on them can be one of the poorest choices in the financial world.

10

What Bonds and Savings Can Do for You

Until a few years ago, I would not have bothered to discuss bonds here. Fixed-income securities were thought to be only for the wealthy, the conservative, and the timid. They were not a way to make money work rapidly. Then came 1979, bringing what may have been the most significant part of the financial revolution we have lived through. Prices in the bond markets suddenly plunged so wildly that this part of Wall Street became a disaster area. Corporate controllers almost lost their grip on the cost of financing their operations. Cautious investors saw huge chunks of their bond values disappear.

Bond prices are apt to look stronger in the period just ahead of us—what I have called Phase I of the outlook. But their prices will tumble again as interest rates soar in the last half of the decade.

Pause for a moment to understand something that confuses even some very knowledgeable people. Bonds are the other side of interest rates. *When interest rates go up, bond prices go down*. Read that over a few times because, otherwise, a few hours from now you will again be tempted to think it must be the other way around. Why don't bonds go up when interest income on them goes up? Because most of the bonds being traded were issued at some time in the past with the promise to keep paying a certain fixed rate each year—say 8% for each $100 that the borrowing corporation or government received. If the rates move up to 10%, no one will pay a full $100 for that piece of paper that pays only 8%. The price will have to drop to about 80 before it can compete with the new 10% bonds coming onto the market.

That is why the bond markets absorbed so much of the shock when interest rates shot up into the teens and then topped 20%. This had been considered unthinkable. Rates used to wiggle by only a fractional amount, and so did bonds. It took transactions involving millions of dollars to add up to a $1,000 gain or loss. Now this immense market with its many billions of dollars worth of paper was showing bigger changes than the stock market.

A Key Figure

What interest rates were really signaling was the sudden fear of financial men that inflation would stay so high for so many years that the dollar figure shown on a bond would have a very shrunken buying power by the time it came due. And the most meaningful single number that anyone could follow was what economists call the "inflation premium"—that is, the inflated interest rate on the closest thing there is to a risk-free obligation, a ten- or twelve-year U.S. Treasury bond.

Such a bond is like a thousand-dollar bill that the holder will be able to spend ten years hence. The interest rate on it should be around 3% because historically 2½ or 3% has been the amount of interest that lenders have been willing to accept from the most unquestioned borrowers—like the U.S. government. Any amount that the rate creeps up to above 3% is called "the inflation premium" because it says that people expect those dollars to be worth that much less by the time the bond matures. As Alan Greenspan has said: In just a few months of 1979, the financial world suddenly decided that inflation by 1990 was going to be 50% higher than anyone had thought.

Then it was that no one wanted to buy a bond anywhere near the old prices. Interest rates went up to entirely new levels, and bonds plunged to new lows. Ever since that time, the slightest signs that might affect inflation or the need to borrow money by corporations, municipalities, or the federal government send bond prices sharply up or down.

The Basic Moves

This can mean several things to you—affecting the exact nature of your investments and the timing of them:

First of all, there is the obvious fact that you will always want to have some cash available, and you should earn the maximum interest on it. The commonest way is to buy a bank savings certificate or to put the cash into a money market fund. Those are two different principles right there because the savings certificate locks in whatever rate is being paid at that moment, while the fund's interest will vary from day to day. If rates move upward, you will be happier to be in the fund; if they slide, you will be glad to have a certificate. Personally, I much prefer the money market funds, which I will say more about in the next chapter, because they give the chance to move cash instantly whenever a better opportunity than simply earning interest presents itself.

Second, if bonds can drop so low when interest rates rise, they obviously have the capacity to climb sharply whenever rates subside. You can capitalize on that without being a professional bond man and trading huge amounts. For there are bond *funds*, which buy a diversified group of bonds just as mutual funds buy stocks.

Your Personal Situation

In any consideration of bonds or bond funds, keep in mind the odd fact that these have become speculative in our era and are, therefore, among the riskier investments. What this means is . . .

- If you are a young person who is interested in some fast speculation, you may find excitement in the bond market, not comparable to options or commodities in the chance of large gains, but more directly linked to your own studies and observations. In other words, if you have a bent for both analysis and speculation, you will find that bond movements are more understandable than most other high-risk situations.
- On the other hand, if you are a youthful investor but want mainly to build wealth steadily for your family's future, you probably can do better in common stocks than you can in bonds. For the long-term holding of a bond is a bet on the eventual buying power of the dollar, and that is not very promising.
- If you are retired or contemplating retirement, you should be constantly aware that bonds are no longer what your father and grandfather thought them to be. Those ancestors used to say that "a good bond is sound as a dollar." That, of course, is just the trouble. You may be able to work out a good and continuing income for yourself by combining some bonds and savings in the ways mentioned above. But never lose sight of the shrinkage in buying power that such an income may undergo. Watch the investment you make, review it regularly in comparison with other alternatives, and be flexible about shifting if you see the trend going against you.

More likely than not, you will elect to invest in a bond fund and let the experts choose specific bonds for you. But the principle followed everywhere in this book is that you should know the basic facts about anything you invest in, so that you can have some feel of whether others are handling your money well or not. So, I outline some of the points an intelligent bond buyer should be looking for, in addition to the obvious quality of the bond—that is, the reliability of the issuer.

- *Is it a long or intermediate bond?* Long-term bonds usually offer higher returns than the shorter issues when interest rates are falling. But investors who want to minimize risk often prefer intermediate maturities, because they are not locked in for as long a time in case their expectations prove wrong and rates rise. The periods when short-term interest rates are higher than long-term rates do not usually last long, and the change that occurs, as the situation reverses, can make substantial gains for holders of intermediate bonds.

• *Is the bond "callable"?* Any time that interest rates are falling, the issuer would like to pay off the debt and refinance it. The holder has an opposite goal: To keep collecting the higher rate as long as possible. Some bonds have a *call* feature written into them—a stipulation that the bond can be paid off any time after a certain date. In that case, the maturity date can be almost meaningless. It may be a utility bond that supposedly matures in the year 2015; but if the utility company has a right to call it by 1985, it will surely pay off the debt as soon as the market conditions make it advantageous to do so. This means a *disadvantage* to the holder. It doesn't make the bond a bad buy, but it limits how much you should pay for it. Knowledgeable investors price such a bond as though its maturity were in 1985 and ignore the stated maturity date.

For the same reason, a Treasury bond maturing in 1990—not being callable—may deserve a somewhat better price, even if the interest rate is a shade less. In other words, the quality of the issue, the rate of interest, and the *assured* life of the bond all have to be weighed into the calculation of how much a bond is worth under the market conditions of the moment.

• *Is the bond already at a big discount?* When rates have been high, there are bonds available at very deep discounts. Coupons of, say, 9% of the original bond value naturally make the bond very unattractive at the issue price of 100. So it falls sharply in periods of high interest rates—no matter how fine its quality. Such a bond might be bought for a price of 50 when interest rates are above 15%. This means that it is very unlikely to be called, because the issuer would not want to pay back a full 100 for it unless rates dropped even lower than 9%. If you buy such a bond for 50, you are virtually assured of the 15% return for its entire life.

Note that the above points apply to those times when interest rates have been relatively high, so that you hope to buy bonds that will rise in value on an expected decline in rates. (There is no need to examine the opposite situation—when rates are low and seem due to rise—for no investor would intentionally buy into such a market.)

Knowledge of these criteria, I repeat, will be useful to you, even if all you plan to do is select a *bond fund,* which buys a diversified group of bonds just as mutual funds buy stocks. These funds have varying objectives and ways of working. So it is up to you to make the original judgment of what type of fund you want depending on what sort of bonds it holds. Once you have done that, you don't have to do the picking of specific ones and worry about relative ratings and safety. The fund does that and gives you a balanced selection, so that even a default on one bond causes little damage.

Among the many highly regarded bond funds are Fidelity (of Boston), Dreyfus (of New York), and Rowe Price (of Baltimore). If you dial 800-555-1212, you will reach an information operator who can give you the toll-free number for each of these funds. Call and ask for full information, so you can compare rates, terms, and records of performance.

EXAMPLE

To get an idea of what returns are possible, let's suppose you put $10,000 into a well-known bond fund at a time when the bond market is at low tide. Its shares—usually quoted as a percentage of 100—are then as low as 95. So you can invest just $9,500 for a collection of bonds that would have been worth $10,000 in better times. Let's say that such bonds are paying a return of about 14% at that time—over $1,400 per year in interest income. At the end of a year, imagine that the bond market has rebounded enough to make your shares worth 99. If you choose to sell at that time, you pocket the $400 capital gain, plus the $1,400 interest; probably more, because it compounds during the year. This will mean a net yield of about 18½% on your original investment. In case the rebound doesn't come about, you still have the interest income, which is more than enough to cushion you against the chance that there might even be a slight capital loss.

"High-Yield" Bonds

I should also tell you about some of the numerous variations on the bond fund idea. The zippiest are a few funds that specialize in "junk bonds," also more kindly known as "high-yield securities." These are issues that have been in default or so close to it that they are being traded at prices like 55, 60, or 70. In other words, a third or a half off their original prices. Whenever a company that has gotten into such a hole makes a comeback and starts paying interest again, that rate is obviously way above anything you get on highly regarded bonds. For instance, a bond that was issued to pay 11% yearly is yielding nearly 19% to any investor who managed to buy it at a price of 60 instead of the original 100. In addition, there is the fact that its value in the marketplace will now rise to reflect the new solidity, and there is the chance of a capital gain of $300 or more for each $600 invested—a 50% profit.

I caution you not even to think of selecting and buying junk bonds on your own. A few bad choices can cost you your entire investment. It is far preferable to invest in a fund that buys a diversified portfolio of such "high-yield securities." Most of these took a beating during the bond market declines of 1980 and 1981. But they did manage to limit their losses, and the potential for big run-ups in better times should more than offset them.

Among the financial groups that have both ordinary bond funds and junk (or high-yield) bond funds are some that were named above. They include: Fidelity Funds (of Boston), Merrill Lynch Corporate Bond Funds (of New York), Oppenheimer Funds (of Denver), and Vanguard Funds (of Valley

Forge, Pa.). Just as I suggested earlier, you should use the toll-free information operator (800-555-1212) to contact each one and ask for data that you can compare.

Tax-Free Bonds

If your income puts you into even a moderately high tax bracket, you may also want to consider a *municipal* bond fund. These bonds are free of federal tax, so that anyone in the 50% bracket who earns 8% on a municipal bond has as much cash left for himself as if he earned 16% on an ordinary bond.

Since most of your ventures into the bond or fixed-income area are largely for the purpose of getting the best possible return on uninvested cash, one of the best-balanced strategies for being sure to lock up a fine return regardless of what happens to interest rates is the one touched on earlier in Chapter 5: *Divide* whatever cash you want to set aside for this purpose into two halves. Select one of the many "families" of funds that has both a *money market fund* and *a bond fund,* and preferably one that allows transfers between its various funds without charge. Either of the two funds is completely liquid, so that you can get your cash in a day if you need to; and if you shop around, studying the ads on newspaper business pages and phoning the toll-free numbers for details, you can find funds that accept as little as $1,000 to open an account. Stick to long-established funds. Others may be fine, but time and experience are your best assurance of safety.

By putting half the cash into the money fund and the other half into the bond fund, you have a perfect stabilizer. If interest rates rise, your income from the money fund will go up daily, while the interest in the bond fund will continue about level, but with a decline in the asset value. The *average* interest on the whole thing will stay very high and certainly higher than any return you could hope for on a fixed savings certificate. If interest rates slacken, you will find that the return on your money fund portion moves down, the interest on your bond fund remains about level, AND the asset value of the bond fund increases. This means that you can sell it for a capital gain whenever you decide that the bond market has done all the recovering it is apt to do. And the total of these three types of return will, once again, be much better than you could do with a savings certificate.

Compounding Power

There is one more advantage to these funds: The income from them can be automatically reinvested and, therefore, keeps compounding. That may not seem like much at first. But even the universal mind of Albert Einstein once expressed amazement at the power of the compounding principal. Unlike interest returns you get directly from owning a single bond, the discipline of letting the income keep turning into principal and earning more income will cause it to build marvelously in the course of some years. Over a twenty-year period, more than *half* of the total return comes from interest on interest. Especially with the divided method explained above, this in itself could be the foundation of an investment system for anyone who wants to put most of his money aside and not work on too many stratagems at once.

However, it is not wise to put your money too long out of your mind. This whole bond market situation creates an illness in our system that is too serious to go on this way forever. Without giving you a dissertation, let me just explain that one basic building block in the way our society works is in danger of crumbling if interest rates keep pushing to high levels.

The savings and loan industry—one that totals about $800 *billion*—is regularly losing ground because a large part of its assets are mortgages on which it earns only old-time interest rates like 8½% or 9%. To finance its operations, it has to borrow current money for much more than that. If current rates don't fall and stay down considerably, the U.S. government would have to bail this industry out. It can't let many savings and loan institutions fail because they are federally insured; besides, such a crisis would be almost as serious as a widespread bank collapse. But bailing out the savings and loan industry would mean printing $50 to $100 billion in new money—just dumping that much more paper into our economy. And by now, everyone above grammer school age is enough of an economist to know how inflationary that is. It would be like throwing in the towel in the inflation fight, admitting that the spiral was about to start again in an even more intense way.

So, watch that "inflation premium." Open the newspaper business page from time to time and see what the current yield on U.S. Treasury bonds of 1990 to 1995 is at the moment. If it starts creeping upward, you can be pretty sure that it is time to have less cash in the bond funds or other fixed securities, more in the money funds, and more in gold and other tangible inflation hedges. If it starts downward, it is time to plow more into both the bond funds and the stock market. This is one of the prime ways that bonds can help to make money for you—not just by the actual cash return on bonds, but by signaling which way a lot of other investment ideas are going to work out.

Here is a brief summary of key facts about various forms of fixed-income securities:

The very safest are those of the U.S. government. They include U.S. Treasury bills, in denominations of $10,000, maturing in 13, 26, or 52 weeks. They are a resting place of money, but not as easily converted to quick cash as a money fund. Such short-term issues—10-year Treasury notes and longer-term bonds—usually pay less interest than long-term ones, although there are odd times when the two rates get inverted. But when money becomes easier and rates drop, these short-term rates usually fall faster than the long-term.

Securities of federal agencies—such as Fannie Mae (Federal National Mortgage Association), Freddie Mac (Federal Home Loan Mortgage Corp.), Federal Home Loan Banks, and Federal Credit Banks—pay up to a full point more than Treasury obligations, while being virtually as safe. They are so closely tied to the federal government that it is unthinkable for them to be allowed to default.

If you plan to hold substantial amounts of cash for a short time, it can pay you to talk to your banker about certificates of deposit, bankers acceptances, and commercial paper. Anywhere from $25,000 to over $100,000 is usually involved. The rate is sometimes negotiated, so that you can actually bargain with a bank to get maximum interest at times when they want the cash badly. This can result in another point or two of advantage over the amounts available on government securities, and the risk is really very slight.

11

Money
Market Funds:
Too Good to be True?

One of the oldest maxims in the financial world is, "When anything seems too good to be true, it probably *isn't* true." Money market funds appear to fall into this category—I have been searching for the flaw that must exist somewhere in their make-up. How is it possible that a brand-new type of investment permits even the very small saver to participate in the kind of top interest rates formerly reserved only for $100,000-and-up accounts? How can these rates be available on a day-to-day basis, so that you can take your cash out instantly without the slightest penalty? And most of all, how can rates of 15% and above go on and on, especially at a time when the inflation rate is only half of that?

It is not possible—not the "on and on" part anyway—for the geometric expansion of savers' cash and buying power at these rates would create a whole new situation in a few years. That much power to purchase or invest would, in itself, become even more inflationary and upset the equation. So something ultimately has to happen. Either the interest rates will simmer way down, or the inflation will increase so sharply that the money balances in these funds will be worth less and less in true value. As you know, my own conviction is that the latter will happen. Many persons—and especially retired ones—have had their lives brightened by the much higher interest income. But retirees more than anyone else need to be aware of the coming facts and to adjust their plans in plenty of time.

As you know by now, I am strongly against the notion of "finding a safe place for your money and leaving it there." There is no such place—least of all any fixed-dollar savings plan, be it a passbook account, a savings certificate, or a money fund.

The reason that money market funds cannot be a permanent money-making machine is easily understood by looking at what had once seemed a similar high-return bonanza: Savings in Mexican banks. They were yielding 15% and 17% when U.S. rates were less than half that much. Many Americans lived beautifully on those returns for years. But the rates were that high because the value of the money itself—the Mexican peso in that case—was suspect. And sure enough, it has suffered repeated devaluations, which pared the value of the capital itself. Earning 15% for five years compounds to just about doubling the original capital. But if the capital itself is then devaluated by a third or a half, you are worse off than you would have been with a lower return on a sounder currency.

The money market funds are not facing a devaluation as such. But the U.S. dollars in which your cash is recorded are going to lose buying power sharply in a few years. So you have to watch for the time when at least the bulk of your money *must* be moved out of cash and into some form that will rise with inflation.

Meanwhile, these funds *DO* represent a marvelous chance to get real returns that are higher than the mass of the people have ever before been able to earn for simply letting someone else use their money.

Start of a New Idea

Why is this suddenly possible, when such funds were unknown merely ten years ago? It was an idea whose time had come. People had been questioning for many years why rich persons and institutions should enjoy much higher rates of return than small savers? Why shouldn't $1 saved on the same terms bring the same *rate* of return, regardless of whom it belonged to? Finally, several persons at the same time had the simple idea of pooling the cash of many persons into a fund that could then buy short-term "instruments" at the highest rates. This means commercial paper backed by big corporations, bank certificates, U.S. Treasury bills, and similar very safe short-term investments.

Soon after these got started, interest rates began to rise for entirely separate reasons. So these savers found themselves earning far more than they had ever dreamed of on the old savings and loan basis. Then as the fund managers gained more expertise, they built the returns up a bit more by means of hectic moment-to-moment trading that takes advantage of every slightest opportunity. Extra cash is even placed on an overnight or 48-hour basis to get the last bit of higher return on it.

HOW SAFE?

The biggest question in your mind—even while enjoying the large new entries that are added to your balance each month—is: How safe is my money? Is it as safe as it would be in a bank or a savings and loan?

It is safer, in my opinion. The fund's operations are watched by a custodial bank. They are not in the hands of a single organization. And the fund's money is invested in a wide variety of assets, most of them backed by either the U.S. government or by firms as prestigious as AT&T, General Motors, and other blue chips. Finally, they are such short-term assets, usually averaging less than 40 days to maturity, that even the pernicious computer embezzler who sometimes drains cash away from banks or stockbrokerage firms would have to keep up daily manipulations at incredible speed in order to cover up his thefts. So losing your money by reason of fraud or mismanagement is a very small risk.

And the fact that money funds are not government insured should not count very heavily, because they are not taking any of the long-term risks that have put the savings and loans into their present unhappy position. The only real cause for concern would be if your particular fund began to try for higher yields than its competitors by buying lower quality commercial paper. There is no sign of this among major funds, but it is a reason for you to monitor your fund's portfolio from time to time. If it gets too go-go, switch to another fund.

Choosing Your Money Market Fund

It is natural to feel a little safer when you see the institution where you put your money, rather than just mailing a check and getting the receipt in an envelope. If you feel that way, your best bet is to ask your stockbroker—or any major brokerage firm—for details on the in-house money fund. You will find that all the big brokers, such as Merrill Lynch, E. F. Hutton, Dean Witter Reynolds, and so on, either manage funds of their own or are closely tied to a fund. They will move money in and out for you on a day's notice, and there should be no commission cost. (Almost all money funds are "no load," meaning that there are no initial charges to be paid. Their operating costs are deducted from the return on investments. So there is no reason for you ever to be talked into paying a fee.)

If you accept the fact that investing close to home really offers no advantages, you are a little freer to compare rates and terms. In that case, think about the few main points that mean the most to you:

SAFETY. Do you insist on the absolute pinnacle of safety? If so, you might feel best with a fund that invests only in U.S. government obligations. There are a number of these, including Merrill Lynch Government Securities Fund, Government Investors' Trust, First Variable Rate Fund for Government Income, Capital Preservation Fund, Cardinal Government Securities, and Sigma Government Securities. They usually pay 1% or so less than you can get from other funds, and I personally do not see the need for insisting on this type of specialization.

MINIMUM. Some funds let you put in as little as $500 to start. Others have a very high initial requirement. And when it comes to adding new amounts there are also variations. If this makes a difference to you, check it out before you choose.

PRIVILEGES. There are differences in the privilege of writing checks against your fund balance. If you like the idea of leaving money in the fund earning interest right up to the moment when you need to make large payments or move cash to your regular checking account, be sure to learn exactly what size checks are possible in the fund you select.

Another privilege that can be valuable is the right to switch without cost from the money market fund to other funds in the same group. This permits you, for example, to move cash into a common stock mutual fund, then back to the money fund for a time, then into a bond fund, and so on. If you are the type person who likes to stay right on top of events and to shift your cash for quick advantages, the right to do it easily and without cost makes it important to invest in a group that offers such diversity.

PORTFOLIO AND PERFORMANCE. Finally, one of the most basic things you will want to know is how well this fund has been performing over a period of time. You can make the comparison by phoning several funds and asking for informational literature. To get a descriptive list of leading funds, first contact the trade association of the industry: Investment Company Institute, 1775 K Street, N.W., Washington, D.C. 20006. Ask for a list of money market funds with as much information on each one as possible. You will find that most have toll-free telephone numbers. To learn the number, call the toll-free information operator: 800-555-1212. She will tell you how to dial the fund at no cost to you.

Just for your general guidance, these following funds have been among the leaders in high yields over the past few years: Value Line Cash Fund, Rowe Price Prime Reserve Fund, Kemper Money Market Fund, Reserve Fund, Cash Reserve Management Fund, and Union Cash Management. But the leadership changes hands often. The yield difference is not great. And you should take all the other factors into account, rather than just going for the leader of the moment.

In case you plan to invest enough and shift enough to want regular updated information, you can consider subscribing to Donoghue's Money Fund Report, Box 411, Holliston, Maine 01746.

When to Put Money In

If you want to do more than just "park" a little extra cash in a money fund—if you want to use fund performance as an active way to make your cash work—there is a method that can give you a keen insight into where interest rates are going:

At least once each week you will find that the financial pages of major newspapers carry a notation of money fund average maturities. This means how long the various financial instruments held by a cross-section of leading money funds still have to run. The significance is this: These money fund managers—some of the keenest students of the interest-rate markets in the world—are constantly trying to sense which way rates are moving. When they feel that rates are about to slide downward, they begin to lock their money into somewhat longer-term loans in order to extend the period that they can enjoy the present rates. On the other hand, when they sense a rising market, they shorten their loans—trying even for two-day and seven-day loans—in order to be able to rotate their cash into more and more lucrative paper as the rise develops.

If you have been noting from week to week that the average maturities were running, say, 35 to 40 days, and then you see a sudden drop into the twenties, be aware that these highly sophisticated money managers are all expecting a period of rising rates. Of course, they can be wrong. But the chances are that they are right: This average figure represents the group opinions and actions of people who are not just guessing, they are on several telephones at the same time, talking with borrowers. When they sense that a demand for their money is building up, they have a strong basis for their conclusions.

This tells you that it is a good time to move more money into the money market funds yourself. The rate of return is likely to be moving higher for a time.

It also tells you to avoid certificates and other instruments that would lock you into a certain position for months or years. Why accept today's rate when there are such strong signs of an uptrend?

Finally, it also serves as general background for stock or bond trades you may be considering. As you know by now, rising interest rates are often depressing to the stock market. Falling rates are good news for stocks. The price level of bonds is similarly affected. If you have buying or selling in mind, let this money fund maturity index help guide you.

The same is true of precious metals dealings, for higher interest rates are also depressing to gold—compete with the attraction of gold and take cash away from that market. Hold off on any purchases of gold when the index tells you that rates will be rising. Accelerate your purchases when rates seem about to fall.

When to Move Money Out

If the average maturities are lengthening and interest rates seem about to slide, you would do best to get most of your cash into something that will lock in a good return for a while. If left in the money fund, it will earn less and less interest with every passing day. So you move it out. But where to? The simplest choice is a six-month U.S. Treasury bill. Whatever rate it offers will be yours for at least that long.

But there is an alternative that gives you the same period of fixed interest and a rate that is usually 1% or more above the Treasury-bill rate. It is called a Unit Investment Trust. A major brokerage firm, most often Merrill Lynch, buys up hundreds of millions of dollars worth of certificates of deposit of foreign banks. Then it sells shares in this "pool" of loans. Because of the new attitude toward such things, the shares are no longer limited to huge investors. You can buy in with as little as $1,000. Many brokerage firms can get these shares for you, even though they originate with Merrill Lynch. But you have to establish a contact in advance because such trusts are not always available. They are usually issued weekly, and they run for six months. Let a broker know as soon as you think you will have money to invest in this way.

For clarity, I repeat that this is not a money market fund. It is a fixed-rate pool and, therefore, more like a certificate you would get from a bank or savings and loan. But this one pays a higher rate, and so it can be especially fine when other rates are sliding.

Your Overall Cash Management

Just to see how all these approaches might work out for you in practice, let's take the following example:

Say you have $10,000 of cash that you see no reason to commit to stocks, bonds, gold, or any other investment just now. You make some comparisons and see that money market funds are yielding about 13% at the moment. You also note in your newspaper that average money fund maturities are getting shorter—most being under 30 days—so you assume that interest rates are due to rise further. You put $5,000 into one general money market fund and the rest into a money fund that specializes in U.S. government securities, just to have the feeling of utmost safety. The former actually pays 13¼%, and the latter 12¼%. Thus, an average of 12¾%.

Watching the average maturities each week, you notice about three months later that they are starting to grow longer. When that happens two weeks in a row, you move $5,000 of your cash out of the general fund, leaving in about $175 in accumulated interest. A stockbroker sells you five $1,000 shares in a Unit Investment Trust for that amount, yielding 12½%.

On the following week, noticing that the average maturities are still lengthening, you move your original investment out of the special government money fund, leaving in $165 of interest. And because you want this part of your cash to be specially safe, you put it into U.S. Treasury notes, paying 11½%.

The trend turns out as you expected, money fund rates come down to the 10% range, and so you are averaging about 2% better than you would have by leaving the cash in its original place. But after six months, you notice that money fund maturities are getting significantly shorter each week. You convert your Unit Trust and your Treasury-notes into cash and put them back into the two original funds. In the next three months, the yields do move up to over 14%. You find that you have averaged slightly better than 13%—over $1,300 in interest—on your $10,000 in that one calendar year. And this in a year when interest rates fluctuated by more than 4%.

With the kind of rates we have been seeing in recent years, this kind of money management could compound to a difference of many thousands of dollars in a few years. Once you start and learn just where to look for the information, it is every bit as easy as checking the daily weather report. A once-a-week look that pays a handsome return.

ENSURING
LONG-TERM
SECURITY

12

Gold—The Misunderstood Metal

A prominent Englishman once sought a private interview with Nathan Rothschild, head of the English branch of that family, and expressed his great happiness at having finally amassed a fortune worth one million pounds sterling. According to this undoubtedly apocryphal story, he wanted nothing more than to preserve it intact. "How can I be sure to have exactly this much wealth to the day I die?" he asked. Rothschild reached into his desk drawer, took out a small pistol, and told his caller, "There is only one way. Use this right now."

Less crisply and less memorably, Rothschild could have advised him to buy gold. For as I have written extensively in scores of publications here and abroad, a lesson that has come down through the ages is this: Precious metal is the only real money in the world—*the only steady standard of value.* It cannot *for long* go up or down in true worth. Distortions are possible for limited periods. But over the years, its buying power stands very nearly still while everything else bobs up and down. And being money, it cannot really be an investment at all. Its function is to preserve wealth, rather than to increase it. That means you have to start acquiring some gold at moderate prices now, but with the knowledge that its great contribution to your well-being will come in the second stage of our economic outlook—when inflation reignites.

To see why this is so, consider what money really is. It is a store of value, of buying power. It has to be something imperishable, savable, easily transportable, plentiful enough to cover the needs of a growing population, but scarce enough to require quite a lot of effort to obtain. And it must be costly to produce. Otherwise, people would just make more of it and spoil its value.

The Ideal Money

There is nothing mystical that makes gold the ideal money; it is merely a matter of natural accident. Nothing else meets all the criteria quite so neatly. Silver has often served the purpose, but its supply is potentially too erratic to keep values steady. Diamonds are not as uniform, not as divisible into smaller units or usable for so many things. And as for paper "money," it is not money at all—only a warehouse receipt for the metal that a responsible government *should* keep in storage.

Gold's one shortcoming is a scarcity that frustrates the desire of popularly elected governments to buy more favor from more voters. If they were to increase the amount of paper money that they print in a very orderly way—in line with the productivity of their economies—they could keep these paper receipts viable and respectable indefinitely. It has been done for long periods. (The British pound, and consequently Britain's government securities, were a steady store of value for most of the eighteenth and nineteenth centuries. There were lapses during wars and financial crises; each time the Bank of England resolutely went back to holding 100% coin or bullion against all notes it issued, making the banknotes "as good as gold.") But in the end, the desire of major governments to please too many people at once results in too much printing of "money." And then, as Voltaire said, "All paper money eventually returns to its intrinsic value—zero."

Those who insist that gold is an outdated relic, and those who believe it to be the perfect risk-free investment are *equally wrong*. There have been times recently when the "gold bugs" who elevate their admiration for gold to the status of a religion appeared to have won. At other times, the American officials who insisted that gold was too volatile to be a standard of value and must shortly collapse seemed to have the upper hand. But in time they will all find that gold is not really heading anywhere. If its value appears to keep trending upward, it means only that paper money is falling further— altering the numbers but not the relative values. The length of a yardstick would not change if officials began to put more line markers on football fields. Neither does tampering with currencies and price tags alter the real value of gold.

The Measuring Rod

Regardless of the dollar numbers affixed to it, one ounce of gold would have bought one good-quality man's suit when this country was founded, or during the Civil War, or when the twentieth century opened. And it buys one good-quality man's suit today. This despite the fact that the cost of labor in the suit has risen remarkably. All the factors of raw materials, labor, overhead, and merchandising become reflected in the single rising figure of "the price of gold." But it is not gold that has a price; gold is what the French call the *numéraire*, the measuring rod by which all other prices are gauged. One ounce of it bought about 15 barrels of oil years ago, and still does—even after great turbulence in both the oil and gold markets. The relationship could change if, for example, the total supply of oil should suddenly swell enormously. But even then, gold's value in relation to the sum total of all world goods would not, *could* not, change appreciably.

I personally believe that this principle has been at work for thousands of years; we have proof that it has been so for at least 420 years. Professor Roy W. Jastram of the University of California, Berkeley has charted the relationship of gold to the wholesale prices of other commodities, starting with England in the year 1560. While these can fluctuate considerably, they always come back into line. Why do they fluctuate at all, one might ask, if gold is so perfect a measure of value? Chiefly because commodities have price swings based on weather, wars, and other factors that crimp the supply, inflate the demand, and so on. The wild rise in 1979 and 1980 seemed to send gold far above the level of other goods, but if the price of fuel is taken into account, gold's rise becomes a normal development.

The steadiness of gold is nowhere so dramatically highlighted as in the hideous German inflation of the 1920's. In 1923, as everyone knows, German marks had become so nearly worthless that people had to take wheelbarrows to market in order to carry the millions of marks in paper notes needed to buy a few groceries.

One person I know who lived through that era had a room papered from floor to ceiling with some of those old marks. And a retired German diplomat, who was a college student in 1923, recalls, "At the start of one term, my father sent me off with money that was supposed to last until the mid-term holiday. When I got off the train at school, that money was worth just enough to make a telephone call—asking my father for much more cash."

The inflation rate had to be counted in the millions of per cent. On Professor Jastram's chart of commodity prices, paper marks zoom straight up and off the page. On the same sheet he shows how the price of those commodities looks when paid in gold—a steady line with moderate wiggles—almost identical to the charts for England and America in those same years.

From 1932 onward, the United States attempted to lock gold at $35 an ounce. Considerable distortions occurred as the world's most powerful government created an artificial level by outlawing gold ownership at home, but promising to sell gold to other governments in unlimited quantities at a fixed price. By the mid-1960's, I was writing repeatedly that this was going to end, that the price of gold and gold-mine shares was going to soar. And sure enough, when the force of gold's attractiveness, at that bargain price, broke America's leaky dam and U.S. citizens were again permitted to own gold, the metal's price soon readjusted. It was heavy gold buying by foreigners that drained billions of dollars' worth of the metal out of the U.S. Treasury at $35 an ounce, and made our gov-

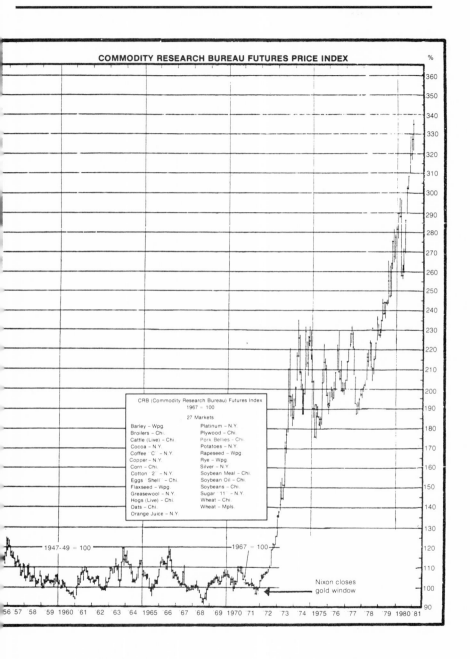

COMMODITY RESEARCH BUREAU FUTURES PRICE INDEX

CRB (Commodity Research Bureau) Futures Index
1967 = 100

27 Markets

Barley – Wpg.
Broilers – Chi.
Cattle (Live) – Chi.
Cocoa – N.Y.
Coffee "C" – N.Y.
Copper – N.Y.
Corn – Chi.
Cotton "2" – N.Y.
Eggs "Shell" – Chi.
Flaxseed – Wpg.
Greasewool – N.Y.
Hogs (Live) – Chi.
Oats – Chi.
Orange Juice – N.Y.

Platinum – N.Y.
Plywood – Chi.
Pork Bellies - Chi.
Potatoes – N.Y.
Rapeseed – Wpg.
Rye – Wpg
Silver – N.Y
Soybean Meal – Chi.
Soybean Oil – Chi.
Soybeans – Chi.
Sugar "11" – N.Y.
Wheat – Chi.
Wheat – Mpls.

1947-49 = 100

1967 = 100

Nixon closes
gold window

ernment admit that its resources were not equal to the world's demand. So the American "gold window" was closed; the fiction that we had no desire to hold gold as part of our reserves was exploded.

More to the point, the purchasing power of gold moved right into its natural place. If we were using gold coins to pay for our consumer purchases, today's prices would look surprisingly familiar to those who cherish a nostalgia for the numbers they knew in young adulthood. A loaf of bread would be 7 to 8 cents, a martini would cost 25 cents, gasoline (even after OPEC had done its worst) would be 10 to 12 cents a gallon, a new Volkswagen would have the $600 price tag that many remember, a new Chevrolet would be $1,250, and the $100,000 home could be bought for under $15,000.

The Underlying Reason

Why this constancy? How can we explain the fact that any one metal has the astonishing ability to keep pace with the whole spectrum of other prices? Easily enough: Only when the cheapening of paper money makes people around the world fearful that they will lose buying power on what they have earned and saved do they turn to gold as a means of defense. To be willing to hold this metal—without drawing interest or dividends—indicates a belief that even a "flat" asset, incapable of growth, is better than a losing one. The demand for gold makes its stated price go up. But whenever conditions improve a little and there seems to be a chance for gains in stocks, bonds, or savings certificates, the yearning for gold ebbs. This movement—approximately paralleling the inflation or deflation of other prices—keeps gold's true purchasing power very nearly constant.

Like all forms of discipline, gold is more often disliked than loved. When the International Monetary Fund introduced its "paper gold," as the Special Drawing Rights (SDR) are often called, many said that it was long past the time when civilized man should have been ready to take charge of the "orderly and rational creation of monetary reserves." Wistfully, we might agree. But we still don't know how to function without gold as a reminder that we should spend only this much and no more.

Why, otherwise, would gold have made its way so quickly back into the center of the world's monetary system? Make no mistake, that's where it is. (Leading officials who try to avoid comment on this in public have often admitted it to me in private talks.) When the member nations of the European Community set up their new European Monetary System in 1979, they agreed to put a large part of each country's reserves into a pool and to issue credits to member governments as needed. And as a large part of those reserves is in the form of gold, the gold will be used to back and to finance each country's spending again. The U.S. Treasury, having once vowed to eradicate gold's place as a reserve asset, had to mumble a few approving words. It no longer has the power to bend Europe to its economic will.

Gold's Uses To You

That this metal can rise or fall sharply for a matter of months, having major effects on speculators in gold stocks or commodity futures, is obvious. But in the course of any given 12-month period, its average buying power will be little altered. So if you simply hold bullion or coins, you will find your own purchasing power similarly static. Not a bad thing at a time when others are seeing their ability to buy shrink daily. Yet not a complete program for financial progress.

Once you have this view of gold's place in the world firmly in mind, you are a clearer thinker on any financial subject. And by making this knowledge the centerpiece of your financial strategy, you will be a more effective investor. The fact that this metal money stands still doesn't mean that it cannot play a *part* in moving you forward. I will show you how gold itself can be used as the safety hedge that allows you to take other risks. The various forms of investment based on gold— coins, mining stocks, old gold coins, Swiss francs, and so on—can often outperform other assets. Most important of all,

GOLD SUPPLY/DEMAND BALANCE

Annual Data

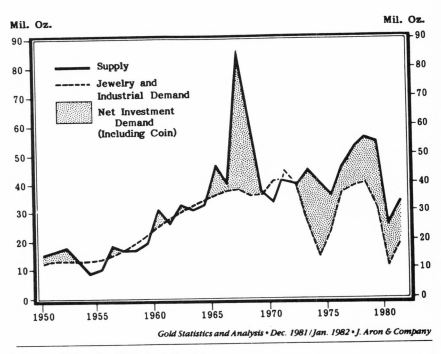

Mil. Oz.   Mil. Oz.

Gold Statistics and Analysis • Dec. 1981/Jan. 1982 • J. Aron & Company

NOTE: *Figures for 1981 are estimates.*

you can make use of what gold does best—which is to tell you where everything else is headed.

Looking at the direction of the gold price—the basic trend over a period of months—is a way of verifying all the other indications of how things are going: It can clarify whether the reports you hear about the dollar's exchange rate abroad are really what they seem. It can shed light on the price trends in other major commodities. It can explain, and to some extent forecast, the relative performance of stock markets in the United States and abroad.

But even without close study, the main fact to keep in mind is that a persistently *falling* gold price is a sign of rising confidence in most other assets—a sign that inflationary forces are at least temporarily abating and that there is reason for underlying confidence in stocks. A persistently *rising* gold price is just the opposite—a warning that many other prices are about to press upward and, therefore, a signal to shift more of your money into investments that protect against inflation.

13

Why You Should Own Gold Coins

Nothing else I write about in this book can be called "an indispensable asset." Only gold deserves that term. Literally everyone should own some.

I have explained the reasons earlier: Gold alone comfortably meets the three criteria that make your holdings both stable and dynamic—ability to multiply in value, stability, and flexibility. It is the perfect hedge to protect all your other financial commitments against the new wave of inflation just ahead of us. The disadvantages of being troublesome to store and insure, and of producing no regular income are more than outweighed by its advantages.

You may be worried by the frequent comment that the U.S. government might one day repeat what it did in 1933 and order you to turn in your gold to the Treasury. By any objective standard, that was a totally illegitimate move, brushing aside constitutional guarantees. So, it is reasonable to fear that our government and others—if faced by a serious problem— might act that way again. But I can find no conceivable circumstance in which such an action would be effective. Besides, I think a growing awareness of the role of gold, vastly greater than it was fifty years ago, will prevent any future president from even trying it. At the very least, I can assure you that it is totally alien to the thinking of the present administration.

The only reason for denying its citizens the right to own this one type of metal is if a government plans, by overprinting and overspending public money, to change the balance within an economy and to redistribute the wealth. In this way, it takes the savings of those who have more and gives to those who have less. Citizens who own gold can avoid this confiscation, since the cheapening of paper money cannot harm them. So a government bent on such a course must first try to remove that defensive weapon from their hands. Today, however, there is a backlash against the half-century of that kind of policy, and it will not die out any time soon.

1933 and Now

Perhaps even more important is the fact that the banning of gold ownership in 1933 involved a special government maneuver that would not be possible now. President Roosevelt fixed the gold price at $35 an ounce, which is estimated to have been $7 to $10 too high for that time. He then ruled that foreign governments could freely take as much gold as they wanted from the U.S. Treasury by turning in $35 for each ounce. The world of that day—sunk in depression—was very short of U.S. dollars. What foreign government was going to give up dollars and buy overpriced gold from us? They did just the opposite: For years, up to and all through World War II, they *sold* gold to us, gladly accepting the over-generous price and taking dollars, which they needed to finance themselves. This *external* arrangement was essential to make the *internal* ruling work; otherwise, distrust of the sharply devalued dollar would have greatly worsened the world depression.

The situation today is the reverse of 1933. Instead of a shortage of dollars abroad, there is a massive glut. Other governments try to think of ways of reducing their dollar holdings. If we again offered to let them have gold for dollars, they would quickly snap it up and take all we have left. The dollar would tumble precipitously on the exchange markets. World trade would freeze up. Whatever economic crisis our president has been trying to cure would seem small compared with the crisis he would create.

So do not be deceived by any argument about gold being "a relic" or "irrelevant to the modern economic system." Almost every government in the world has become increasingly gold-conscious and tries to hold some of it as its prime asset of last resort. That is what gold will be to you too—the asset that puts a firm foundation under all your finances.

Coins Are Best

I have used the term "gold" in a general way, but you will now be wondering how and in what form to own some of this metal. And my very strong recommendation is that you acquire mainly what are called "bullion coins." That means they are pure gold coins that have no special rarity or collector value. They are simply gold bullion that some government has minted into coin form, so that their value is just slightly higher than the per-ounce cost of gold in bars. This premium is small enough to be negligible. So you can compare and keep track of your investment by just noticing the current gold price as it fluctuates daily.

Coins, in my view, are preferable to bars of gold bullion. The reason simply being that they are smaller, and they make your gold more easily divisible. If you were to buy, for example, a one-kilo gold bar, you would be investing $10,000 or more in a single transaction, allowing no room to acquire a little at a time and "average in" if the price level should be very volatile at that time. Then if you should need some cash or have any other reason for wanting to sell a part of your gold, you would have to decide to sell all or nothing. In contrast, coins can be bought even one at a time. The price is usually a little better for larger purchases—say ten coins at a time—but the difference is slight. When you think of selling, you can also do it piecemeal. As far as the premium is concerned, it really has little bearing. You may pay 4% to 6% more for gold in coin form, because a manufactured product naturally always costs more than a semi-manufactured one. But that premium is still there when you sell, so any disadvantage is minimal. Besides, you are not about to become a trader in gold. You are going to buy some, perhaps add to it over a period of time, and hold on to it for a very long time. A few per cent added to cost is less important here than in any other form of transaction.

Rare and Not-so-rare

Anyone who is interested in coins will wonder about two other categories whose value is not strictly tied to the bullion content:

- Rare coins, whose investment possibilities I do not at all want to downplay. Far from it. Many of these have outperformed the ordinary coins whose value resides only in their metal. But it takes special know-how to deal sensibly in the numismatic field. If you already have it, you are fortunate. If not, you would need to study extensively from books on the subject, many of which are in your public library. And it would be equally important to keep up with current developments by regularly reading *Coin World*—a newspaper for numismatists—or other leading periodicals in the field.
- The special or commemorative new issues that are marketed with very aggressive hard-sell tactics. These are neither rare coins nor bullion coins. Whether they are privately minted or issued by governments, they must be warily viewed. The chief criterion has to be: How much gold do they actually contain and what are they worth on that basis alone?

One set of four coins put out by the government of the People's Republic of China has just been mentioned to me on the day this is being written. The total weight is two ounces of gold with a fineness of a little over .91. Just over 1¾ ounces of pure gold total, worth about $700 at the moment. But these coins are being sold for $2,400. And they are being touted as a great investment, partly because they are a limited edition. The inference is that masses of collectors will bid up the price in the months and years after they are issued. Why should they? The series is nowhere near that limited. Only if the price of gold itself triples will these coins become a *breakeven* proposition. Breakeven, mind you, while any genuine bullion coin that was originally purchased for its intrinsic value will be tripling the original investment.

There can be exceptional commemorative issues, but it takes study and patience to find them. For example, the Royal Canadian Mint produced a beautiful coin a few years ago to mark the new national anthem, "O, Canada." It contains one-half ounce of gold and is 22 karats, being alloyed with silver, which gives a lovely lightness of color. The perfectly-made proof coins are sold in relatively small quantities—only about 100,000 a year—and this gives considerable assurance that the price will at least hold its own. Over the course of years, it is likely to gain in value. But you must still be aware that new production is coming along to supply part of the demand, so it is unrealistic to expect a sharp price jump.

Anything really rare—usually meaning quite old or a coin that had a unique flaw at the time of minting—can indeed be an exciting buy. But anything that is "limited" only by the conscious decision of an executive, an official, or a committee is very unlikely to be rare enough to do the buyer much good. You can be sure that the issuer is putting out as many of them as he believes the market will easily absorb. The judgment may occasionally be sufficiently far off to allow a modest price rise after issuance, but nothing more. If you stick to a rule of paying no more than 8% premium over the current gold value of the coins you buy, you will miss few opportunities—and save a lot of money.

At Any Time of Life

How much of your total assets should be in the form of gold? This naturally has to vary according to your personal situation.

I suggest you think of 20% as a round figure for *all* your precious metal holdings. If these include gold stocks or silver, the amount devoted to coins may be scaled down proportionately. In any case, a minimum of 10% of all you own should be in gold coins. The frequent argument that these do not work for you—do not earn current interest or dividends— is a reason to avoid putting too great a part of your assets into gold. But it is not at all a valid objection to this much of a commitment because the gold "anchor" that gives your finances so much steadiness, allows you to do other things that will more than make up for the small amount of interest that you pass up.

If you have a high regular income and keep adding a little gold each month or each three months, you will gradually accumulate a hoard that will astonish you with its value at some later date. Even the most restricted investor—the retiree on a tightly fixed income, for example—should have some gold in coin form. That way, if soaring prices make your pension, your savings certificates and the interest they pay suddenly seem too skimpy to keep you going, you will find your coins doubling or tripling in value. Your overall buying power will be propped up. And in place of desperation, you will have the assurance that just selling one of your coins at carefully spaced intervals would keep the bills paid.

Five "Best" Coins

Turning now to the kind of coins you should favor, there are five: Krugerrands. Canadian Maple Leafs. Austrian Coronas. Mexican pesos, in various sizes. English Sovereigns. There are others that fit the description of bullion coins, but they are not as commonly traded. This makes them a little less liquid, less easily sold. The five I have mentioned are universally known and accepted, easy to find and buy, easy to sell if you need to.

The Krugerrand has become the most popular of all. The reasons are not very important ones for all bullion coins are essentially just ways of buying gold in convenient sizes and shapes. But the characteristics that gave the Krugerrand its quick lead over other coins are worth knowing about. First, it is minted by the Government of South Africa, and apparently many investors have the impression that gold from the world capital of the goldmine industry is a little more trustworthy or desirable. This is not true, but there is no sense in arguing with success. The other reason is more to the point: The Krugerrand contains exactly one troy ounce of gold (although it weighs more because it is alloyed with copper), so anyone who holds it knows exactly what his coins are worth as soon as he hears the day's gold quotation.

There is now a "mini-Rand," also minted by South Africa, which weighs exactly one-tenth of a troy ounce. It is also gaining popularity, and it enables people to buy gold with an even smaller investment. The premium is a little higher still. So aside from owning a handful for possible use in the kind of economic emergencies that have sometimes forced people to live on their gold, there is not much point in having any large quantity of the smaller coin.

The Canadian Maple Leaf is also minted by a country that produces gold of its own. In fact, the emphasis on using only new gold from Canadian mines is one of its unusual features. The Maple Leaf has made slower progress with investors than the Krugerrand, but it has been gaining favor. It also is guaranteed to contain exactly one ounce of gold, but it weighs less than the Krugerrand because it is not alloyed with any other metal. The Maple Leaf has two particularly attractive features:

- Fineness. It is guaranteed to be .999 pure gold. In order to be sure that every coin meets that specification, the mint aims for even greater purity—.9999—and most of the coins hit that mark. Not a major factor in normal times, but potentially important in a period of crisis. If you had to sell off a coin for living purposes, its fineness means that a dentist, jeweler, or other artisan could use the gold without refining it, so it would become more desirable.
- Slight extra gold content. The Canadian government guarantees that each Maple Leaf contains *at least* one

ounce of pure gold. Since variations have to be reckoned with, a little more gold is included to meet that promise. So 100 of these coins really contain slightly more than 100 ounces of gold.

Neither of these points means that an investor should pay much more premium for a Maple Leaf than for any other bullion coin. But surely they are reasons why the Maple Leaf should be worth at least as much as any other one-ounce coin—why no other should command a higher premium.

The Austrian Kroner (often called Corona) contains just a shade less than a full troy ounce of gold—.9802 to be exact. The only slight disadvantage is that if you know how much an ounce of gold is selling for, and want to know how much your Coronas are worth, you have to multiply by .9802. They are an excellent buy because of this slight deviation; and the fact that fewer investors are acquainted with them results in the lowest premium of all. They can sometimes be bought for only 3% or 4% over the value of their bullion content.

The Mexican fifty-peso piece is the heaviest of this group, containing 1.20564 ounces of gold. Despite this irregular amount and the larger investment required, it commands a premium nearly equal to the Krugerrand in the United States, because it has been known here for a long time.

Finally, the **English Sovereign** is unique in many ways that may interest you. It is the smallest of the entire group, being only .2354 ounce—or just under ¼ ounce of gold. Since it became a very widely used coin around the world in Britain's imperial days and, in fact, used to be minted in several different locations throughout the Empire, it has a historical standing that no other bullion coin can match. Its acceptability at any bank or coin exchange is the very highest. These facts combine to make it a worthwhile addition to your gold holdings.

But more care must be taken in buying Sovereigns than any other bullion coin, because the British Government, after an interruption in 1968, began minting Sovereigns again in 1974. This means there are "old Sovereigns" and "new Sovereigns." Even the old ones are far too common to be considered collector's pieces, but they do command a premium of 25% or more. The newer ones have a smaller premium, so you must be sure not to be charged as though they were older coins.

Where to Buy

This brings up the fact that it is important to buy coins from the most reliable sources possible. To accomplish that, follow two rules: Buy only from well-established firms, never from itinerant dealers. And compare prices between at least two sources, preferably three. Even more important than not being overcharged is not buying any "bargains"—for there is no such thing as bargain gold. It is money, and nobody sells it at a discount. One of the main reasons for careful comparison of quotations is not only to get the best sensible price, but also to be sure that you do not fall into a counterfeit trap, which is rare, but not unheard of.

Three reliable sources that I know well are the following:

Investment Rarities, Inc. 1 Appletree Square Minneapolis, Minn. 55420	800-328-1860
Intergold Corp. P.O. Box 12096 Albany, N.Y. 12212	518-459-4084
Republic National Bank 452 Fifth Avenue New York, N.Y. 10018	212-930-6515

If you have an established dealer in your own city or nearby, you should certainly ask him for price quotations. But also compare his price with the prices from one or more of the above. Don't worry too much about any disadvantage of dealing with distant sources because the arrangement is very simple. You place your order by telephone, then send a check for the agreed amount. Within a few days, you will receive the shipment by registered mail. If you should want to sell at some future date, you again make the deal by telephone, wrap the coins securely, and take them to the post office. It is very little harder than dealing with a local firm.

One thing I recommend strongly is to try to keep working with a single dealer if you should make a series of purchases. It is a great advantage to have a business relationship of this kind, in case you should wish to sell. Bear in mind that the dealer also has a problem of making sure that he doesn't accept fake merchandise, so he may charge you for examining and assaying any coins you try to sell him. This problem is at least eased if you say the coins were bought from him to begin with. He can't be absolutely sure that they are the same ones, but, if you have made repeated purchases, he is likely to take your word.

Keeping Gold Safe

Finally, there is the question of safely storing and insuring your coins, which is the only real problem in the whole matter of owning gold. Its worth is beyond question. Its value will not disappoint you over the long run. Only if it is stolen can you lose.

Obviously it is most important that you do not keep your gold at home. Do not imagine that any hiding place is clever enough to foil thieves; with metal detectors, they will find your gold wherever you conceal it. So either a bank safe deposit box or a lock box in a very secure storage building is essential. Some form of insurance is also required. You must be aware that no bank insures or guarantees the contents of a box that it rents to you. The bank doesn't know what you put into it, so it cannot honor any claim from you in the rare event of a theft. The only way to plug this gap, wherever your gold is stored, is to buy an insurance policy. This can be fairly costly, but special rates are given when the coins are in a safe deposit box.

Investment Rarities, Inc., mentioned above as a coin dealer, offers a special rate of $150 annual premium for $50,000 worth of insurance on gold and other precious metals. That is the maximum amount for the contents of any one box, but you can insure for a greater amount by having your metal in more boxes. To compare their terms with what is quoted by your insurance agent, write to: Monetary Protective Group, Investment Rarities, Inc., 1 Appletree Square, Minneapolis, Minn. 55420. Or phone 1-800-328-1860.

For the Bold or the Wary

Once you have taken care of these three points—selected the coins you want to hold, started a purchase program, and decided on a safe way to store and insure them—you will have a tool that can be used with a variety of other techniques to form profitable combinations. That is on the positive—the aggressive side of a financial program. Let me emphasize, however, that this reserve of gold is every bit as vital for the retiree or for any other person whose situation calls for maximum restraint and caution. If you believe that you cannot afford to devote any part of your capital to a static investment in gold, ask yourself whether you can afford to gamble your entire future without any insurance against the great possibility that worsening inflation will attack and decimate everything else you own during the second half of the 1980's.

So the first phase is the time to start acquiring gold and building your holdings, even though the attractiveness of other investments will tempt you to wait. By the time new inflation rears in, gold will have moved up a very long way. Those who are prompt to act will have a great advantage over the majority who rush to buy later.

14

Gold-Mine Stocks—For Income and Appreciation

Unless you are in a very high tax bracket and want to avoid investments that bring taxable income, I urge you also to consider owning shares in some of the leading gold mines. The reason is this: A balanced position in both gold coins and gold stocks gives you a good chance of earning some income on your money, making eventual capital gains, and enjoying stability in the difficult years beyond 1985.

Your gold coins will probably pay no dividends or other regular return. In fact, they cost a little to store and insure. If you have an equal amount invested in the stocks of really fine gold mines, these can pay as much as 16% to 20% annually in dividends. Meanwhile, they also have some aspects of owning gold itself, for their reserves of ore underground will keep rising in value over the years. The combination of coins and stocks will work out to 8% or 10% yearly income from your total investment in gold, which is very high for an asset with so many other advantages.

Even more important, the split between coins and stocks provides you with protection against the one thing that worries some investors about the gold-mine shares—the fear that South Africa might have a racial upheaval bad enough to destroy the production facilities of the mines. I do not regard this as likely; but since I am talking about the part of your portfolio that is supposed to provide the greatest security, I must lean over backward to protect you against every contingency.

Well, if there were political catastrophe in South Africa, the cut-off of gold production would result in a soaring gold price because the world's supply would be totally inadequate to balance the demand. So your gold coins would gain greatly in value—probably enough to offset the decline in the worth of your gold stocks. Here again, we are setting up the closest thing this world can offer to a can't-lose situation. You are essentially hedged, protected, insured, and still you have the kind of profit potential that usually goes only with high-risk investment.

Buy Mines, Not Holding Companies

If you ask a broker for advice on South African golds, and he is unsophisticated, he will probably suggest that you simply buy ASA Ltd., which is the largest holding company specializing in South African stocks. Or he may suggest another such firm, like Precious Metals Holding Co. Any of these are like buying a mutual fund that selects and buys a good many gold-mine shares. As you know from other chapters, I often favor the use of a fund to do your stock or bond selecting. It also offers great diversification. But in the case of gold, I can see no reason for buying a holding company. Their dividend payments are a small fraction of what the individual mines pay—for apparently management expenses soak up the rest. The skill and knowledge that is usually required to make selections is rather irrelevant in this case because there are so few top-notch mines. Once a fund purchases a group of these, it has very little more to do. So I say buy them directly, save the management costs, and collect the big dividends for yourself.

Quite a few of the major brokerage firms have analysts who study the South African shares closely enough to help you greatly in making your choices. If you have an account with any such house, just ask your broker to get you the latest recommendations from their gold analysts. One firm that does a particularly fine job is Drexel Burnham Lambert, Inc. Its precious metals department goes into the conditions of the gold-mine industry and individual mines with great care. If you have access to one of its offices, you should ask to see their studies.

South African and Other Mines

I write about *South African* gold stocks because those are far and away the leading ones. They supply nearly 700 tons of gold per year out of a total world production of about 950 tons. Their ore richness completely overshadows anything else in the world. If you like the idea of speculating in small gold ventures, there is always the outside chance that some developing mine in the United States or Canada may have stock that will go from 75 cents a share to $7.50. Such percentage gains exceed anything you can hope for with sounder investments; but they are gambles, and there is no way to fit them into a logical investment plan.

Some analysts, who deserve to be heard, also like the idea of owning the American firm, Homestake Mining Company, or the more diversified Dome Mines, which has large holdings in Canada, as gold investments that would do exceptionally well in case the South African mines were shut down or threatened. These companies have ore of relatively low grade, so you are buying advantageous location rather than really rich resources. I don't object to seeing a small part of any portfolio invested in that way, but it should not be enough to detract from the main plan, because the chance of continuous high returns is very small.

So I will concentrate on the relatively small group of South African gold stocks that are the world's principal suppliers of this unique metal. In few other fields is the cream of the crop so easy to find, and the daily performance so neatly concentrated in a few newspaper lines. *The Wall Street Journal,* for example, has a small box headed "Other Markets," and a section of that list is marked "South Africa." It contains little more than a dozen names, and every one of them has something to recommend it as a mine with unusually large ore reserves, unusually long life, or unusually high annual dividends. These are mines that you can buy here in the form of ADR's—American Depositary Receipts—meaning that one of the leading New York banks actually holds the shares, collects the dividends for you, deducts any applicable South African tax, and so on. As far as you are concerned, the ADR certificate you get is just like stock, and the dividend check you receive is in U.S. dollars.

There are a few other major mines that do not appear on that list. They are traded mainly in London. Some newspapers carry them separately, either in their general list of over-the-counter stocks or in a group of British securities. *The Wall Street Journal* puts them under the heading of "Foreign Markets." Your broker can buy any of these for you just about as easily as he buys an American stock. There is nothing difficult or "foreign" whatever about buying and holding these shares. The mines are located in South African places with exotic names, and the Johannesburg Exchange is the home bourse where these stocks are traded; but a great deal of the activity in the ones I am about to describe occurs in London and New York.

Driefontein—A Super-Mine

If one were looking for the U.S. Steel or the General Motors of the gold-mine industry, the choice would probably be a mine called Driefontein Consolidated. It is a super-mine—made up of separate areas that are long-established, very large, and is by far the most profitable gold mine in the world. Although it has historically used a very high grade of ore, it shifted to some of its lower-grade areas in recent years in order to be flexible and adapt to the changing gold price. You should also know that many mines have veins of gold ore of varying quality. When gold's average price rises, they can use their low-grade material fairly profitably, hold their earnings and taxes down, and save their best ore for later.

Driefontein's stock has ranged between roughly $20 and $33.75 per share, and its dividends have been around 12%

in the more lucrative years. Now that the eastern and western sections have merged, this mine's estimated remaining life is about fifty years. Bear in mind that such estimates are often extended as the gold price trends higher. Whenever there is a big move in the gold stocks, up or down, Driefontein has a part in it.

But . . . it is not wise in the case of gold stocks just to pick the industry leader and buy only that one. There are often times when some mines develop better than others, so that a diversified group of stocks has a better chance of getting in on a spectacular performance. Then there is the fact that either fire or flooding in a single mine is possible. It doesn't permanently end the mine's value, since the gold ore is still there. But it can close down operations for months and cost very heavy sums to repair—making that one stock very weak for a good while. So it is important to hold enough different stocks to lessen the effect of any such setback.

Vaal Reefs—Another Leader

Another of the very great mines is Vaal Reefs Exploration and Mining Co. It is large and sprawling, has high-grade reserves in several areas, and can look forward to over twenty years of life, which is considered in the "long" category. Vaal Reefs produces nearly 10% of all South Africa's yearly gold output (and an even larger part of the uranium production, on which I'll comment later). Its stock has ranged from $36 to $150 per share in the past three years, and its annual dividends have been as high as $17.50.

Kloof—A Special Advantage

I want to mention Kloof Gold Mining Co. next, even though it is not among the very largest. It is well-endowed with reserves that give a long estimated life—well over twenty years. And being a relatively new mine that began operations only in 1968, the equipment is modern and efficient. There is, however, the added special fact that Kloof had some serious problems a few years back which held down its profits and the price of its stock for some years thereafter. The sinking of shafts was more difficult and costlier than expected, and an outbreak of fires took a further toll. The troubles have been overcome at very heavy expense, and this can be an advantage, because work to ensure against new setbacks has already been done, whereas other mines that never had these problems might not be as well prepared if they struck. Kloof's price in the past three years has ranged from $13 to over $70 per share, and annual dividends have been up to $6.

Several other stocks should be mentioned as paying excellent dividends, while still having life expectancies that are respectable or better. These include: President Brand Mines, President Steyn Mines, St. Helena, and Free State Geduld.

I should explain that high dividends sometimes are characteristic of old and dying mines. The dividend then is almost entirely a payout of assets, as it is to some extent in the case of any company selling natural resources. Its products, unlike manufactured goods, cannot be renewed endlessly, so the dividends are only partly profit and partly a sell-off of its reserves.

But some mines pay out high returns while still having an estimated life of fifteen, twenty, or more years ahead. This makes them excellent for retirees and other persons who need more annual income, but a little less interesting for those whose financial and tax situation makes it preferable to see the money reused to enhance future gains. Make it a point to note the dividend policies and history of each mine you study, and set that against your own income and tax situation.

Short-Life Mines

Shares in mines that are expected to have only a few years of remaining life should not be despised. For one thing, they often pay out enough to provide a fair return on the investment before they die. For another, they can suddenly discover new veins of ore in adjacent areas and get a considerable extension of life. Finally, even without such discoveries, their life and profitability may be increased by a rise in gold prices. Every mine has gold ore remaining when it finally ceases operations; it is simply a matter of how much it costs to extract an ounce of gold from the grade of ore that is left. If the average gold price moves up considerably, extraction that had been unprofitable can suddenly become very desirable.

Three examples. A combination of such factors has made many declining mines even more lucrative than some of the rich ones in recent years. Welkom Mines, for instance, was selling at prices like $3 and $4 per share in the 1970's. Shareholders were often getting nearly 20% return on their investment, but with warnings that this might go on for only a few years. After the 1979–1980 jumps in the gold price, the shares went to nearly $30 at times. The mine that was once expected to be dormant by now is still spoken of as having "a limited life prospect."

Another ailing patient that has confounded the mourners is Doornfontein. Erosion in an important area of the mine seemed to have brought its life to within four or five years of its end. But by shrewdly acquiring rights to approach the area from another direction, the company may have extended its survival to twenty or more years.

Perhaps even more dramatically illustrative of this principle is Free State Geduld. Ten years ago, its stock was selling at about $12 a share, despite 20% and higher dividends, because its life span was thought to be only ten more years, at best. Now, having ranged in price as high as $130 a share and paid out annual dividends of over $12 in a single year, it has expanded and extended operations under skillful management. And it is spoken of as being potentially in the long-life category, with twenty or more years of milling low-grade ore ahead. Such ores could, of course, become increasingly profitable as the price of gold rebounds.

Gold plus Uranium

Most of the above mines I have described are on *The Wall Street Journal's* main list headed "Other Markets" that I previously named. Although the second list contains mainly mines that are less known in the United States than they are in

Britain, two outstanding ones in it must not be overlooked: Hartebeestfontein and Harmony. Both are big, solidly endowed with ore reserves, giving them a medium life expectancy of fifteen to twenty years, and are also the owners of considerable uranium. This is a point to consider in choosing the gold mines you want to own. Although the price of uranium has been a disappointment in recent years because environmentalists have prevented the full development of nuclear energy, its future is beyond question. More uranium at higher prices is the outlook. So the mines that have it do offer still another resource that will add up to profits and dividends of a high order later on.

For the speculative-minded person, there are numerous other mines that could be of interest in a different way. These are the ones that are priced low because of a short or uncertain life situation. Among the ones that fall into that category are Blyvooruitzicht, Bracken, Leslie, Loraine, Marievale, Stilfontein, and Witwatersrand Nigel. They can sometimes work out very profitably in case of a sudden jump in the gold price that makes their low-grade ore more lucrative, or if the management succeeds in arranging a merger deal with another mine that works to the advantage of shareholders. A few knowledgeable speculators even succeed in gaining handsomely from shares of mines that are in "the break-up category." They pay a price that is thought to be the minimum value of the remaining equipment and land rights, but there are often happy surprises that greatly enhance the lingering worth of the old mine.

Even if you do have the inclination to study such unusual deals, only a small amount of cash should be diverted to these high-risk situations. They are not at all a part of what gold stocks are all about. So no such speculation should be considered a part of your precious-metal portfolio or allowed to detract from the commitment to finer mines. *Those* are not a speculation. Their ore reserves are part of the real money that you hold for the highly inflationary future. They will look very attractive in the next two years and truly spectacular in the middle and late 1980's.

15

The Silver Roller Coaster

Whether your interest is mainly in speculation or in patient investment, *silver can be a very attractive asset for the period of high inflation ahead of us.* It combines short-run volatility with long-range growth. And it offers the average person a way to get in on precious metals with a relatively modest amount of cash.

This can include cautious investors and retirees who have very little leeway for taking risks. You will see in this chapter that small sums can be put into silver investments over a period of time, so that the drain on your other finances is slight and the average cost is likely to prove very favorable.

Before telling you the various ways to deal in silver, I will give you some background on silver's place in the financial world. It will be useful to go back a little, not just because silver has an interesting history, but because remnants of the older situation still greatly affect the present-day price behavior of this metal.

Silver was once much more of a competitor of gold. Many nations considered it worthy of being used as a base for their currencies. That was true in the United States, where "bimetallism" was long a political issue. There were two main reasons why some Americans insisted that both gold AND silver should back our money. A narrow reason was that people living in silver-mining states naturally wanted to see their product given the greatest possible prominence and held at the highest possible guaranteed price. A broader reason was that this wider backing for paper money would permit more money to be printed, tending to expand opportunities for the lower economic class and to erode the assets of the wealthy. In other words, it was an early form of the liberal versus conservative tug-of-war.

The Historical Price Ratio

A century or so ago—and for some decades after that—silver was valued at about $1/16$ the price of gold. Sixteen-to-one was thought by many to be almost a law of nature. But it did not last. The main reason for the change was simply a more plentiful supply. Anything that is discovered in great enough quantities will go down in value. This is even true of gold, which caused a wild inflation in Spain when large supplies of it poured in from the New World. But great new supplies of gold have never persisted enough even to keep pace with the larger demand of growing populations. The supply of silver has mushroomed at times, so that whenever both silver and gold have been allowed to move freely on financial markets in recent years the price ratio has usually been between 30 to 1 and 35 to 1.

While the nineteenth-century controversy involving silver was primarily political, the modern struggle is mainly commercial. It has been between the producers and the users of this metal. Naturally enough, the states that produce silver have urged their congressmen and senators to press for measures that tend to support the price. But a trade association of manufacturers who use silver—such as the makers of tableware—has lobbied hard in Washington to oppose this price-propping.

Each side has had its share of success. At one time, the creation of a government stockpile (which some critics insist was far larger than we could ever need in a wartime crisis) helped to keep prices fairly firm. Then the decision to sell off some of this hoard brought fear of a price collapse. Actually, the sales had the opposite effect. A huge silver stockpile had been seen as an overhanging supply that might inundate the market whenever the government decided to let it go; when speculators saw that the pile was being reduced and that the market absorbed it without falling apart, they gained a new confidence in the future of silver.

As of now, the world's current production of silver is *less* than current demand. In other words, there is a potential shortage. But the accumulated hoards of it—including some still held by the U.S. government—easily take care of redressing the balance.

Besides, technology has taken a hand in the silver situation far more than in the case of gold: Scientists of the photographic film industry, and especially of Eastman Kodak Company, have developed ways of reclaiming much of the silver from old film at very low cost. They have been extremely close-mouthed about how much of this they accomplish, wanting to keep their competitors in the dark. But it is clear that a lot of silver supply-and-demand figures never show up on financial pages or as transactions on commodity exchanges. X number of ounces simply move from one Eastman Kodak plant to another.

The Great Move

These and other price depressants led some of the world's top metals traders to conclude, in the early 1970's, that they might never see the huge price surge they had long expected. One of these men said exactly that to me in London one day: "I've been bullish about silver for so long—always confident about the fundamentals—and I've been disappointed year after year. So I have decided not to be bullish any more." Famous last words, of course. A few weeks later, the price of silver on American commodity markets began to edge up, then jump up, and suddenly the move became front-page news. Some mysterious buyers were moving in with purchase orders of fantastic size, apparently heedless of price. At last, it was learned that the oil-rich Hunt brothers, backed by Arab resources, had decided that silver was the world's most under-priced commodity and were accumulating unheard-of quantities.

As silver doubled in price, then went on to $5 and $6 per ounce, the possibility that it might go even to the incredible $10 level was forecast by some, but scoffed at by most analysts. It went right through that figure and gathered speed on its astonishing rise to almost $50 per ounce.

Speculative fevers of that kind always break and give way to a price collapse even steeper than the rise had been. A different reason is given in each case. This time, it was the desperate action of the commodity exchange where silver is traded—first in raising the margin amount to a level traders could not meet, then in actually prohibiting any new buying. Of course, a market that can have only sellers and no buyers is going to come down in a hurry. The Hunts complained that they had been unfairly booby-trapped and forced into billions of dollars in losses.

There is something to be said for their claim, for there are few games in which it is considered proper to keep changing the rules simply because someone is winning. But if that had not caused the price to tumble, something else would have. Because people who had never dealt in precious metals before had begun to buy at the highest prices. And when that happens, it is only a matter of very little time before professional traders get back to their senses and start taking their profits.

So silver fell and fell and fell. It leveled off around $13 or $14 for quite a while. Just as it had been said once that silver could never pierce the $10 barrier, it was now being said that it could never go through that level in a downward direction. It did.

Three Points to Remember

The whole cycle reconfirms some valuable lessons that you should keep in mind. Not only for dealing in silver, but for any kind of trading.

- Markets always over-react and over-correct. We have seen both silver and gold move far too high and fall too low within a very short time span. So *never* assume that a given price level cannot be pierced. Even if your judgment proves to be right about the long-run price, you can lose on a quick trade because markets often go far beyond reasonable levels.
- No person, no industry, and no government can suppress for long the fundamental dynamics of an important commodity. Blocking its natural movement simply builds up pressures that will cause some very *unnatural* movements for a period of time.
- Everything in the financial world is related to many other things. Silver was not moving entirely on its own when it surged or when it fell. It was moving partly because gold was moving; in turn, gold was moving because the price of oil was soaring.

These reminders can be helpful to the investor, and are absolutely essential to the speculator. With silver's past and present in mind, let's look at the practical ways for an individual to make profitable use of its future prospects.

When, How, and Why to Buy Silver Coins, Bars, Options, Futures

The world's total production of silver is less than the total demand for it. If you recall the fact that important stockpiles are being eliminated rapidly, you will see that we are approaching the time when there will be no more old silver to draw on. This means that there will be a persistent seller's market—a situation where those who are trying to buy silver have to work harder than those who offer it for sale. So the price will be bid up higher and higher. This is the *why*, the reason to buy silver and hold it. The price IS going up.

How high? Probably to $20 and above by 1983, and well beyond that level by the middle of the decade. I firmly expect that during the 1980's it will penetrate the old highs and move on toward the $100 mark.

SILVER COINS

The simplest way to move into this metals market is by buying what are called silver junk coins. The unfortunate name should not lead anyone to despise them. It refers to U.S. dimes, quarters, and half-dollars that were minted before 1964 and, therefore, are of silver, rather than the later mixture of metals. They are called "junk" simply because they sometimes come in bags containing $750 face value of a *mixture* of these coins. In recent years, they have ranged in price from 8 times to more than 20 times the face value of the contents.

It is not necessary to invest ten or twelve thousand dollars in an entire bag of such coins. Just a few coins can be bought at a time. Any of the dealers named in the chapter on gold coins will quote you prices on these, and you can compare them with the offerings of dealers in your own locality.

You will have to take the same storage and insurance precautions that were suggested for gold. Do not keep any substantial quantity of these coins in your home, or even buried in your yard. There are too many persons with metal detectors who scour neighborhoods whenever they see that the occupants of houses are away. A safe-deposit box is well worth its modest cost.

SILVER BARS

These are a somewhat cheaper way to buy this metal, but they are bulkier and less easily used. Many of the same dealers who sell coins also offer bars of silver in various sizes. Since the price relationship between coins and bars varies from time to time, it is wise to ask for prices on both and then decide which to buy.

Incidentally, there is a way to profit from this changing relationship, and it is risk-free. Oddly enough, it is possible only when silver you already own is falling in price. If your silver coins drop well below the price you paid for them at some point, you can sell them, and use the proceeds of the sale to buy silver bars. Because the coins sell at a premium over the price of the silver bars, you will get more ounces of silver than you had before. AND your loss on the coins can be taken as a tax deduction. Take this example. Let us say that you own 1,000 ounces of silver in "junk coin" form. It cost you $12,000 when silver was selling for $12 an ounce. Now the price is down to $8.50 an ounce, and your coins are worth about $8,800. You sell them for that price and find that you can buy 1,050 ounces of silver in bar form for the same amount of money. More importantly, you take a $3,200 tax loss.

This kind of transaction has to be carefully weighed against your own present and future income picture. You do have to keep in mind that the silver bars now have a much lower cost basis, so that a profitable sale in a later year could create a higher tax liability. But it is excellent if you have rather high taxable income this year which may diminish in future years.

SILVER OPTIONS

You may occasionally be contacted by a dealer who offers silver options or other forms of contract that bet on the future price. I suggest that you say a firm no to all of these. Some are honest, some are not; and it is hard to distinguish among them. But even with a perfectly reliable dealer, you are getting into a considerable gamble. You will be asked to put up several thousand dollars in the hope that the silver price will advance a certain amount within a given period of time. If it fails to do that, you can lose some or all your cash.

SILVER FUTURES

Anyone who wants to speculate on the future price of silver can do it more cheaply on the commodity futures exchange. There are full contracts of 5,000 troy ounces and mini-contracts of 1,000 troy ounces. These smaller ones are a good way to get started and get the feel of precious metals trading, even for persons who have the means to go into the larger contract. By putting up only $500 to $1,000—depending on the exchange rules of the moment and your broker's own requirements—you can control $10,000 worth of silver when the price is $10 per ounce. Remember, you may be called to put up more cash if the price falls and cuts your equity. It is very unwise to go into such a speculation unless you are prepared in these ways:

First, you have studied the present silver price and its trend and assessed all the reasons why it should go lower or higher. If, for example, you see that the price of oil appears to be rising again, you notice that gold is trending upward, and silver has not yet made a similar move, there is reason to think a rise may be just ahead.

Second, you have a definite trading plan. That is, you are not simply going to buy one silver contract, hope for the best, and get out if that first try is a loss. A reasonable plan could include a decision to start with one mini-contract and then add more of them at certain fixed prices if the metal goes lower. You might, for instance, buy one more contract for each 50 cents of decline. You would be moving your average price lower with each new purchase; but bear in mind that you would also be having to put up more margin to cover the $500 loss on each mini-contract that such 50-cent drops represent. That brings us to the next absolute requirement . . .

Third, you must have enough easily available cash to cover this entire plan—the margin needed for each added purchase and the extra margin to cover price declines down to whatever point you set as the place where you would quit trying and sell out your whole position. Depending on just what points you decide on in advance, this probably calls for $5,000 to $7,000 of money that you do not plan to need or use for any other purpose.

You will see from the above why I consider patient long-term investing in silver coins to be preferable for most individuals and certainly for those on fixed incomes. Although your group of futures contracts might net you a gain of ten or twenty thousand dollars if silver suddenly turned up strongly, the chance of losing everything you put up has to be faced. On the other hand, putting $5,000 into silver coins a little at a time—perhaps starting with $1,000 worth, then "averaging up" and buying added amounts, if the price advances, or "averaging down" and buying at lower prices, if there are drops—you could turn a $5,000 or $6,000 profit if the silver price doubled. Not as dazzling as the profit on futures contracts, *but accomplished with very low risk.* Silver's eventual price gain is virtually certain, so it is just a matter of waiting—with no danger that anyone will call you and demand additional cash. The only "loss" you have to reckon with is the lack of interest on your capital during the time you hold the silver. But even at high interest rates, one good capital gain outweighs many years of interest earnings.

Silver's great appeal, in my opinion, lies in the fact that it can be bought in small quantities, a little at a time, built into a substantial holding without making a great dent into your other capital, and held with the confidence that it will make healthy gains in the inflationary "second stage" of our economic outlook just a few years away.

This makes it excellent for all investors: If you are young or middle-aged, even small amounts of silver will grow to important sums long before the various times in your career when extra cash is likely to be needed. And if you are already retired, it is equally attractive because it safeguards your other assets against inflation losses, apart from offering the chance of capital gains that would greatly improve your position.

Some pessimists want to own silver coins because these would be the easiest money of all to use for survival in a time of chaos. But the more pleasant fact is that silver—like gold—will not need chaos in order to rise in value. As stockpiles dwindle and demand continues to outpace production, its price will go much higher even in the best of times. The average price you pay for it in the coming year or two will come to seem very low one day.

IV

UNUSUAL WAYS TO MAKE YOUR MONEY GROW

16

Options—Safe Ways to Buy and Sell

Options can involve big risks or almost none at all, depending on the technique you use.

When traded as most persons do, options are bets, pure and simple. Although they involve some of the same judgment that is used in selecting a stock, they add all the hazards of a *race* because you can be absolutely right about the fundamental worth of the stock they represent and still lose all your money. Any short-term dip in the overall stock market or temporary bad news for the company is likely to kill all chance of recouping the cash you put up for a buy option. If you had bought the stock itself, you could just ride out the setback and later see it turn to a profit. But an option can be like a bet on a horse that starts to run well only when the race is ending. You just tear up your ticket and forget it.

Why then does anybody trade options? Because the leverage is incomparable. The chance to turn tiny amounts into big ones is not matched anywhere else in the financial field. It is possible, though rare, for a few hundred dollars to become several thousand within days. And for that to occur within weeks is not at all unusual.

The fact that this doesn't happen to most people—that most options expire unused and therefore with 100% losses—proves that the usual way of gambling on options is poor business. BUT . . . there are ways of making options a conservative part of your program for beating the new wave of inflation. In particular, there is a way to play this game and still be absolutely sure of at least having all your money back by the end of any given year. This makes it worthwhile to discuss options here—to give you the necessary background to consider my own unique method of trading them. For I think it is one of the most direct ways to aim for large returns and still sleep soundly at night.

What Is an Option?

Before outlining the few simple steps that make this possible, let me explain the basic facts about options that will already be known to some readers.

An option is the *right* to buy or to sell 100 shares of a certain stock at a set price and by a given date. It is not stock in itself. It has no value once that date passes. But during the period of its validity it gives control of that stock—the right to deal in it or to pass it up. And for that right you pay a premium. The amount can be quite hefty if you buy a new option with, say, six months of life left. And it is even more if the set price is near the point where the stock is now trading. Because the chance that you will be able to use the option profitably is greater. Conversely, the premium may be small or minuscule if the option is within ten days of expiring or 20 points away from its profitable level. Like betting on any longshot, you put up a very little bit, are likely to lose it all, but just *might* collect a 1,000% return.

First, a few quick examples to show how this works:
On a day in October you decide that Mobil Corp. common stock, now trading at 26, should go much higher. But you think it may take three months for the move to come, so you look at options that expire in February. There are some February 25's, meaning that they give the right to buy the stock at 25—even lower than its present price. But they are quoted at 9, which means you have to pay $900 plus commission for an option covering 100 shares. Very costly, but that is because the option is already "in the money"—that is, it can be used

even now to buy the stock for $1 per share less than its current price. So anyone who owns the stock is not going to give away cheaply the right to buy it below market value, perhaps to benefit from a big jump in that value over the next three months.

You decide to go for something less expensive—the February 30's. They are selling for 5¾—$575 plus commission. If the stock does as well as you expect, perhaps moving up to 45 before February, you can use the option to buy it at 30 and instantly resell it for 45—a gain of $1,500, less the option price and commissions. You will probably net about $875 on a $650 investment. When accomplished in three months, that represents over 520% per year rate of return.

But . . . let's suppose you have two brothers. One of them is a more aggressive risk-taker than you are. When you mention the Mobil Corp. to him, he buys the *November* 30's. Bearing in mind that this is already October, he is shooting for a very rapid run-up in the stock—OR an almost immediate loss of his investment. But because the time is so short, his investment is tiny. The option is selling for 1¼. He puts up $125 plus commission for each option contract, and he decides to buy ten of these options. If the stock jumps up to 34 before his expiration date, he will make about $190 on each option, or $1,900, within a week. If not, he loses nearly $1,500. Let us hope he has some substantial capital gains for the year, so that part of this loss can be recovered by a tax deduction.

Your other brother is cautious and often gloomy. He questions the outlook for the stock market in general, for the oil stocks in particular, and more especially for Mobil Corp. The more he looks at your proposition, the more he feels like going the other way. He thinks of selling Mobil short. But that holds unlimited risk, for if it goes up and up, there is no telling how many thousands of dollars can be lost.

So he decides on a *put* option—the right to *sell* 100 shares of stock, rather than to buy it. The principle governing premiums is much the same as on *call* options. That is, the longer the life left, the more the premium will be. But whereas the call option is more expensive when the price is set low (the right to buy cheaply), the put option costs more when the price is set high because it gives the right to sell at a high level.

If your gloomy brother is right and Mobil falls to 16 within his option period, the right to sell it at 30 will give him a very neat profit. Just how much depends on what premium he paid, and note this: There is no strictly fixed rule on premiums. It depends on how much some unseen seller of options is willing to take for this right you are after. He may be another private investor like yourself who owns Mobil and wants to make some additional premium income by selling options on it. Or he may be a professional who feels he knows enough about the company to sell "naked options"—meaning that he risks a heavy loss if he is far wrong because he must then buy the stock at a higher price in order to deliver it to you.

The Selling Side

The fact mentioned earlier—that most options expire without being exercised—reveals that the sellers of options are usually more knowledgeable than the buyers. They collect a lot of premiums for selling bits of paper that are later torn up and that never require them to deliver anything. And this opens up another way to earn money in the options market: *Not* by selling naked options, which should be left strictly to the professionals—and even some of those have gone broke in a single day. But by selling options on stocks you already own.

Suppose, for instance, that you have 2,000 shares of Mobil Corp. common stock. You like it. You don't have much fear of suddenly wanting to bail out. Let's also suppose that you originally bought it for $15, and you would be quite happy to accept $30 a share for it. Now, with the stock at 26, you tell your broker to *sell* ten call options covering 1,000 shares—half of your holdings. You sell six-month Mobil 30's at a premium of 10, so you collect $1,000 less commission on each option. Ten of these give you about $9,200 net.

If the stock shoots up to 40, you may regret having to let 1,000 shares go at 30; but your remaining 1,000 shares are making you happy. More likely, however, it will not go up strongly enough to make the option buyer take the stock away from you. You keep all your stock and any dividends that were paid during that period, *plus* the $9,200 of premium income. Quite a few investors and many large funds are now using this as a way of earning additional cash.

There are innumerable ways of developing more and more complex approaches to option trading. The examples given above are some of the simplest. If options intrigue you, any brokerage firm can give you literature that explains ways to trade "option spreads," where you buy a long call option and sell a short one, or you buy an option at one price level and sell one of a different price on the same stock. These usually give less leverage, more modest potential profits, but with much reduced risk.

A Fully Insured Method

In my opinion, the ideal way to play the option game is the risk-free one that I mentioned earlier in this chapter. It goes this way: Decide, first, how much of your capital you consider to be available for stock *speculation*. Note the distinction that I do not mean all your stock investment funds. Not the kind of money that you are putting into companies with great long-term growth and earnings potential. But the smaller amount that you had planned to plunge with if your broker or your favorite financial journal mentioned some special situations that seem likely to give quick profits. Let's say that you have set aside $10,000 for that purpose.

Now figure how much interest you can earn on that in one year at the highest-yielding source you know. It may be a money market fund currently paying 14%. If you hold aside $1,200 and deposit just $8,800 in such a fund, your capital will be back up to $10,000 in one year. The $1,200 is what you use to speculate in stock options. *In other words, you just borrow the interest income that will be building up day-by-day and gamble only that and nothing more.*

It may be argued that there is still a potential loss because

$10,000 at the end of the year won't have the same buying power as it did twelve months earlier. But there are hair-splitting answers to that, too; such as the fact that if you lose the $1,200 in the option market, part of it is recovered as a tax deduction. The point is that you take money that was intended all along to be risk capital and you subject it to far less risk than would have been true in the stock market.

What kind of options do you now proceed to buy with your $1,200? That depends on your personal bent. You can go for the high-risk, high-return options; or you can play more conservatively. Most of the experienced traders I know would counsel you to "buy time rather than points." That is, be willing to pay a little more premium in order to gain another month or two of life in the options you select, and make up for it by buying options whose premium is reduced because the fixing price is quite a way off from the present market value of the stock. Paying a lot for options that are close to the present stock price can cost you dearly, because a market setback may suddenly make these far less desirable pieces of paper. But the amount of *time* you buy can never dissipate in a flash. It will go a day at a time—always eroding the value of your option, but also giving the fresh chance that today will be the one when a takeover bid or a new-product announcement makes the stock move up a dozen points.

The one firm recommendation I would make on what type of approach to take with your $1,200 is *to diversify*. Don't put it all into one situation, however attractive.

Bear in mind that making big money on options relies on buying something that others in the market have not recognized. When you consider how many highly sophisticated persons are culling every stock—and how many of them have access to facts that you may not have—the chances that you will move in the right direction before they do are not great. But if you have four options, they are four times as great as if you select only one. If each of these has an average life of, say, two months, there is a fair chance that one of those 60 days will bring good news for just one of your choices.

Having some of your options in the form of puts and some in calls gives a further safeguard; this way, even an overall market turndown does not preclude the chance that you will have at least one good trade. That is all you need in order to make this approach worthwhile. An $18 stock that goes to $38 while you hold a couple of call options on it can run your $1,200 up to $4,000, even if your other options all draw blanks. You can then diversify that amount and try the same thing over and over—as many as five or six times in the course of a year.

A clever options trader might well increase his original $1,200 to $5,000 by the time his basic hoard in the money market fund had also grown back to $10,000. With remarkable luck, he might do two or three times that well.

So it is at least possible to double your money while assuming virtually no risk. Double or nothing is a foolish gamble; at some point, it always turns out that nothing is what you are left with. But double or stand pat is the risk-taker's ideal.

I know of no financial approach that is more attractive arithmetically than this one, and I urge you to give it careful thought. Don't let the apparent complexities of options trading frighten you off. You can learn the basic facts from a small brochure that your broker's office will be glad to give you, although it will take a good bit of time for the knowledge to become second nature. After that, the main thing is to be very firm about staying within your strict limit on how much money to risk on options. Only if you stray beyond that are you in real danger.

The goal of every investor is to find a method that gives the highest potential return with the lowest risk. This one is *it*.

"Why, in that case, not just do this with all your capital and forget the rest?" There is a very important answer to this question. The approach offers the *chance* of earning at the highest rate—not the certainty. The only sure thing is that you need not be badly hurt. But if you happen not to have the knack or the good fortune to see your options prosper, you will wind up with only your original cash. And that will not be good enough in the inflationary times to come. So a variety of approaches is needed to be certain that you will move ahead financially.

17

Trading Commodities— Even for Conservatives

"I know a retired man who ran $17,000 up to over $400,000 in three months by trading gold, Swiss francs, and German marks."

"Yes, but I know one who was left with a half-million-dollar debt he can't pay because Maine potatoes went crazy while he was short."

These are typical stories in the unpredictable commodity trading game—the wildest game in town. Not even in a gambling casino can so much money be made or lost in minutes. And yet, on the basis of my own first-hand experience, I can assure you that:

- Some conservative investors actually use the commodity markets as a way to protect their savings.
- Cautious businessmen buy or sell commodity futures to insure against changes in the cost of their operations.
- Out-and-out speculators can judiciously manage their trades to make steady profits.

The commodity trading game is played five days a week with billions of dollars—in metals, grains, meats, currencies, and wood products. For the most part, what traders actually swap are agreements called "commodity futures," rather than the goods themselves. A futures contract for March soybeans, for example, means that one party agrees to buy and another agrees to sell 5,000 bushels *next* March at a given price. Both parties usually sell out their positions long before March comes. Eventually, on a certain day in March, the actual soybeans must be exchanged, but the rights will have changed hands countless times before that. In most instances, a contract is resold within days, and often, within minutes. Commodities traders seldom even see the products they trade, much less have them delivered to their door.

Transactions are made electronically between the chief markets of Chicago, New York, and London. (Kansas City, Minneapolis, Toronto, and Winnipeg also have important markets for some commodities.) An office in any major city of the Western world can place an order and have it executed within minutes. On the trading floor itself—the "pit"—the terrific pressure makes all deals gentlemen's agreements until confirmed on paper at the day's end.

What Is Leverage?

In the rapid-fire world of commodities trading, a price change of just a few cents can mean a difference of thousands, even millions of dollars. For not only is the trading incredibly fast, but there's also an explosive effect called "leverage."

Leverage means that just a little money can control a large contract, multiplying the chances for gain or loss enormously. A deal to trade 5,000 bushels of beans for $7 per bushel means a contract totaling $35,000. So a change of 20 cents a bushel works out to a $1,000 difference.

The amount of actual cash required to swing such a deal varies with the commodity, its volatility, and the brokerage firm involved. But the range is from as little as $700 up to just $2,500; for a bean futures contract as described, it might take $1,500 to make the trade. That means, for $45,000, a speculator could control 30 such contracts worth over $1 million.

Speculators who trade in and out during the day can gain or lose many times their original capital. Leverage makes it possible to lose much more than you could at Las Vegas or Monte Carlo, because losses can go far beyond the money you put up. They can mortgage your entire future.

Conservative Trading

As Morton Shulman wrote in his book *Anyone Can Make a Million,* "Commodity futures represent the quickest possible way to get rich or go bankrupt . . . Here is probably the only completely honest form of pure gambling in the market." How can there be any conservative side to such a game?

First of all, no one is more eager than your own broker to save you from big losses. If you lose more money than you have, it's his firm that has to make it up—and it could take the rest of your life to pay it back. So the rules are fairly rigid for either putting up extra cash or selling out if the market goes against you. Any competent broker will insist that you place protective "stop orders" to get you out of the market before your loss becomes catastrophic.

Having and sticking to a firm system is another safeguard that is considered essential for conservative trading. No trader I know has succeeded for long by relying on feelings or hunches. There are two types of approaches—widely different—but unified by the idea that a plan works only if it's allowed to proceed without tampering.

The **"fundamental trader"** knows all that can be learned about crop plantings, weather conditions, domestic and foreign demand for the particular commodity that interests him. If it is wheat, for instance, he has even assessed the crop outlooks of Russia and The People's Republic of China, so that he knows how much they are likely to buy from Western sources. If he decides that total world demand will far exceed supply, he buys contracts that control future wheat. If he can afford to, he buys more, even when the price falls, confident that the market must go his way in the end. His gains can be very large; his risk is great. But if he is a real pro, he makes sure that losses are limited to an amount that won't put him out of business.

The "technical trader," on the other hand, pays little or no attention to fundamental conditions. He believes that market action tells the most about what will happen, and tries to get aboard a trend. But it takes tremendous patience to keep from jumping the gun, to wait until a trend has established itself. Usually such a trader will follow the numbers, buying or selling only when prices hit certain points. This may mean buying a commodity only after it has risen quite a lot—just when others think it is time to sell. He must intentionally forgo all the profits that might have been made on the way up, in order to feel assured that the market is really pointing toward much higher peaks. More often than not, the bandwagon will indeed keep moving after the technical trader has jumped on. Since such traders always have protective stops just a little below the market level, their risks on any one speculation are relatively small.

So patience, oddly enough, is one of the most important traits for success in this fastest of all markets. "The thing that defeats lots of traders," says commodity professional Anthony M. Reinach, "is that they cannot resist deviating from styles that customarily win for them. To stick to a winning style requires patience and perseverance. Very few can trade every day and emerge winners."

Futures Contracts As Insurance

Even more conservative than the systematic traders are those who have a particular interest in a commodity—as a farmer or rancher does—and who use the commodity markets for their original purpose—as a hedge against price changes. Farmers are almost always sellers of futures, selling, sometimes as early as planting time, some or all of a future crop to lock in a current favorable price. Selling short helps farmers with banks as well, for bankers prefer to lend to those with a sure thing rather than to "gamblers."

The farmer's customers may also use futures for insurance.

A familiar example is that of a baker who naturally uses great quantities of wheat flour. He knows that any big jump in the price of wheat can hurt him badly in case a competitor has bought up cheaper wheat in advance. So he buys contracts for wheat six months ahead. If the price does go up sharply, he'll make enough on the futures contract to offset the higher cost of wheat flour. If it stays level, he's no worse off. If the price goes down, he loses on the contracts, but saves on the cost of his flour. In any case, his small commission cost—each broker sets his own commission fees, but they average $70 to $100 for a "round-trip" (buy and sell) trade—is like an insurance premium to guarantee that he can keep his bread competitive.

"I'm using that same principle to make my construction business less vulnerable," a Washington contractor told me. "When I was clearing a piece of land for a new office building, I knew that rising interest rates could add three to four percent to the eventual $4 million mortgage. That could mean $120,000 to $160,000 more interest each year—enough to make my whole project look sick. So my accountant suggested that we sell interest-rate futures. Up to that time, I didn't even know that such things were swapped as commodities. I told him, 'Look, I'm no gambler. I'm a builder. That sounds like a crap game to me.' It took him hours of explaining to show me that the real gamble was in *not* trading futures. By selling U.S. Treasury bills futures or Government National Mortgage Association futures short, I was locking in my interest costs now. Rates did rise. The mortgage on my building is 3½ percent higher. But I have a $250,000 gain in my commodity account to offset it."

Similarly, builders may trade lumber and plywood futures to assure themselves an even break on their materials needs. Textile firms often buy or sell cotton futures. A number of jewelers and dentists I know buy gold contracts. The real goal is to *avoid* speculating, in effect, to guarantee today's prices for tomorrow.

Even if you determine, as most people do, to avoid commodity trading altogether, try to understand how the markets work. Commodity trading is a huge and increasing part of our financial picture. In 1978, 45 million futures contracts were traded in this country. It jumped to 90 million by 1980. And the estimates are 250 million by the middle of this decade. The trends in these markets can point significantly to the direction of the whole economy. So you are personally affected, even if you never trade.

If you *do* decide to trade, your choice of a method is all-important. Unless you have expert knowledge or a normal business interest in some field that involves commodities, you should not even give a thought to trading them on the fundamental basis. You are at too great a disadvantage than those who know far more and sooner than you do.

Say you go on a vacation trip and see unusually plentiful corn crops growing on every side. Some speculators use that as a reason to call their broker and sell corn short. They assume that such a huge crop is bound to cause a surplus of corn and send prices way down. They may be perfectly right. A small information sample of this kind often does tell a much bigger story. But before acting on it, a well-rounded speculator would have to know the crop outlook for the entire country—AND the entire world. For if Russia is having a disastrous year and suddenly announces plans to take quite a lot of our surplus off our hands, there will be a big jump in prices.

It would also be important to know how much of a corn carryover there was from the previous year, how much the price had already declined to reflect this year's big crop, what the outlook is for competitive grains, and many other related factors. Even the strength or weakness of the U.S. dollar would play a part, since a weaker dollar makes our products cheaper to foreign buyers, encourages exports, and, therefore, tends to push corn prices here at home *higher*.

With Help or On Your Own?

For the nonexpert, then, there are only two reasonable approaches to commodity trading: One is to put some cash into a *managed commodity account*, if you learn of a solid, highly reputable brokerage firm whose trading executive can show a long period of successful management. This means putting up a substantial sum—at least $10,000, and some account managers insist on $50,000 or even $100,000 minimum—and allowing the executive to trade it as he chooses. A few such money managers have shown average gains of 30% to 40% over a period of several years. But they are always careful to warn you that past performance is no guarantee of the future. There are inevitable periods of loss. All responsible firms have a flat rule that they close out your position and return what remains of your capital in case the equity falls too low—usually to about 25% of what you first put up.

Obviously, no one should go into such an arrangement with cash that is vital to his future. It is only for people who are prosperous enough to mean that any capital loss is shared with the U.S. government. In case you do decide on this way of trading commodities, ask to see a great deal of evidence of the account manager's past performance, and find out exactly what trading system he uses. If you are told that it is a combination of technical charts and personal judgment, be very wary. This usually results in scrambling both systems and producing nothing in the end.

The other approach is to *learn a technical system yourself*—one that allows you to keep numerical records of commodity prices and to use them as signals to buy or sell. I will give you an idea how to do that because it may help you decide whether you belong in commodities at all. Also, the knowledge would be useful if you should put your money into the hands of an account manager but still want to understand what he is doing with it.

A moving average is the basic tool for technical trading. It begins with listing the daily prices over a period of time and dividing them by that number of days to get the average price. The easiest way is to use each day's *closing* price and to keep what is called a "simple moving average." This means that each day you drop the price of the oldest day and add the latest closing price; in effect, substituting the newest information for the oldest, as shown in the example below. In the second column of figures, you delete the number from Day 1 and add the closing price of Day 6:

DECEMBER COPPER—5 DAY AVERAGE

Day 1—	85.25		
2—	87.30	Day 2—	87.30
3—	85.70	3—	85.70
4—	86.80	4—	86.80
5—	86.80	5—	86.80
	431.85 divided by 5	6—	87.60
	= 86.37		434.20 divided by 5
			= 86.84

You would not actually start trading after such a short time. A few days' figures do not represent a trend. At least several weeks of keeping averages on a variety of commodities should be allowed before actually putting up any cash.

In the most elementary approach, a speculator plans to buy whenever the price of copper touches or exceeds the average on the way up and to sell when it touches or falls below the average on the way down.

In order to give a simple example of how this might work, let's assume that the figure of $86.84 resulting from the second list is a satisfactory one and that you have decided to buy copper whenever the closing price goes more than 100 points above that average (the figure of 100 being an arbitrary amount that you may adjust on the basis of your experience).

That means you would actually buy on the next day, Day 7, because the price goes as high as $87.86—102 points above the average. You would then "stay long" copper, meaning that you would hold your position and not sell, until the day when the closing price falls below the moving average. If you are fortunate, that day will be some weeks off as shown in Chart A, because it is those long trending periods that create the big profits. Such a lengthy move would almost surely mean that the metal was moving upward rather consistently and that any pullbacks were quite small. By that time, the higher and higher closing prices would have moved the average to a figure well above $90. The copper that you purchased at $87.86 might be resold for $94—a net gain of over $1,500 on each contract.

Chart A

If your decision has been to trade either long or short—that is, to reverse your position and bet on declines at certain times when the trend seems to be downward—you would sell not just one contract when the sell signal finally occured, but *two* contracts. One sale would liquidate your profitable earlier purchase; the other would make you "short one copper," meaning that you have sold copper you never owned and will now hope for a price drop so that you can buy it at a lower price. Since I mentioned before that this is December copper, you have until that month to complete your trade. But it is always wise to liquidate a position before the first day of the contract month because after that the trading often gets hectic and price movements can be ragged as some other traders rush to buy or sell before the last moment.

The Whipsaw Problem

Careful studies have shown that this simple moving average method, when used on a wide variety of commodities simultaneously, yields very substantial profits—perhaps even greater than those of more sophisticated systems. *But it has a serious flaw.* It can move you in and out, from long to short, every few days. Small losses in each case, but potentially so many that you would suffer considerably before one really long move provided a big gain. The whole aim of any technical system is to create good profits with minimum risk. The very quick moves involved in a simple five-day system do ensure that you would buy or sell right at the start of any trend; but they can also subject you to a series of whipsaw experiences with rises or drops that did not prove to be the start of anything.

If, for example, copper had been trading higher before that $85.25 close on Day 1, you would undoubtedly have been signaled to sell when it came down to that point. You might have had to buy back and reverse to a long position on the upmove of Day 2, but then flipped over to the short side on Day 3. Each of these trades would have cost you about $600 loss per contract. It may well be that the rise on Day 4, moving you again to the long side, will be the start of something big—perhaps sending copper to 110 and giving you a $5,000 profit per contract. But relatively few traders can afford all the losses that pile up along the way before that happens.

Smoothing the Action

So there are many variations to "smooth" the performance of the average—aiming to take advantage of its ability to signal large moves while avoiding the false signals as much as possible:

The simplest smoothing method is to make the average a weighted one, giving more weight to the recent prices and less to the older ones. The rationale is that a commodity's performance of the past still has some importance in the overall picture, but that its recent trading pattern is even more important. In this case, the copper average we looked at earlier might look like this:

$$
\begin{array}{rrcl}
\text{Day 1---} & 85.25 \times 1 = & 85.25 \\
2\text{---} & 87.30 \times 2 = & 174.60 \\
3\text{---} & 85.70 \times 3 = & 257.10 \\
4\text{---} & 86.80 \times 4 = & 347.20 \\
5\text{---} & 86.80 \times \underline{5} = & \underline{434.00} \\
& 15 & 1298.15 \text{ divided by } 15 = 86.54
\end{array}
$$

The higher average number that this yields (86.54 instead of 86.37) is likely to delay a buy signal. It might diminish your overall profit a little if the move proves to be a good one, because you would be paying more for the copper. But it also tends to prevent your getting any signal at all if the move is going to be a loser.

There are even more sophisticated ways of smoothing the performance. Most of them consist of adjusting the average to get figures that experience has shown to be better predictors of the future trend. And some traders use a combination of two moving averages—one a five-day fast average, like the one described above, and the other a much slower average, often twenty-day. The trends of these are plotted on a graph. And whenever the short-term average crosses the longer-term average in an upward direction, it is considered a buy signal. When the five-day average crosses the twenty-day average in a downward direction, it is a sell signal.

These methods produce more limited profits than the potentially explosive gains that can come from plunging into situations in gambler fashion. The more you smooth the method, the more you limit the gains. But the term "limited" is deceiving. An average gain of 30% to 50% annually is quite possible, and that would hardly be called "limited" in any other field. At that rate, $10,000 turns into about $14,000 in one year, then into nearly $20,000 in the second year, $28,000 in the third year, nearly $40,000 in the fourth, and over $50,000 in the fifth year. At these levels, the annual increments get to be really substantial.

Numbers Win over Hunches

One of the hardest things about using a technical system is finding the discipline to stick to the numerical approach when it will so often seem to clash with your common sense.

You will hear, for instance, that the outlook for cotton is miserable—a large crop and a poor chance of selling much of it abroad. Yet your index tells you to *buy* cotton. You calculate the possible losses and quickly phone the broker to cancel your buy order. This one time, the decision to override your own averages may be right. The signals are correct no better than 40% of the time, at most. But it is also possible that many other traders who have sold cotton on the basis of its "miserable" outlook are about to start taking their profits. A great many people *buying* cotton contracts in order to liquidate positions can push the price up 700 points easily.

As I have pointed out in connection with other types of markets, the worst aspect of using hunches or snap judgments is that your judgment is probably right, along with that of many other equally bright minds. When all those people start to take their gains or cut their losses, the sudden price explosion up or down can turn a correct judgment into a catastrophe. So your judgment may add up to a big loss, while your arithmetic may—against all visible logic—give you a $3,500 profit.

If your decision is to keep your own charts and trade independently, get at least one, and preferably more, of the published books on commodity trading. These will give you more details of each system and enable you to select the one that suits you best. A very good primer to start with is *Winning in the Commodities Market*, by George Angell, published by Doubleday & Co., Garden City, N.Y. If you want to add more sophisticated thinking, there is an advanced book called *The Fastest Game in Town*, by Anthony M. Reinach, published by Random House.

Whatever you decide, do not make the amateurish mistake of thinking only in terms of buying, not of selling short. The downside is fully 50% of the commodity markets. Even some professional managers say that they always play only the long side—partly because all short sales are taxed as current income, while long trades can turn into capital gains. This is poor reasoning. Any gain is good, regardless of taxes—and some of the biggest gains come from short sales. If you select someone to manage your account, be sure he does not have this antishort sale philosophy.

Holding on to Your Gains

Finally, don't allow success to be your undoing. Commodity trading can sometimes seem to go so well that you are tempted to throw all system to the winds and plunge ahead. Your original capital of, say, $10,000 may suddenly mushroom into a $25,000 equity and tempt you to double your bets—to buy two contracts of each commodity instead of the one contract that you had thought you could afford. But success in any system runs in cycles. It is most vulnerable after a big win, so any expansion should be done with great care.

THE NAMES OF THE GAME

Commodity futures traded. Metals: copper, silver, platinum, gold. Grains and feeds: wheat, corn, soybeans, soybean meal, soybean oil, oats, rapeseed, rye, barley, flaxseed. Livestock and meat: cattle, feeder cattle, hogs, pork bellies, iced broilers. Foods and fiber: fresh eggs, Maine potatoes, coffee, sugar, cocoa, orange juice, cotton. Financial: Mexican peso, Swiss franc, British pound, Canadian dollar, Deutschemark, Japanese yen, Government National Mortgage Association, U.S. Treasury bills, Treasury bonds. Wood: lumber, plywood.

Contract. Purchase or sale of one unit of a given commodity. For most grains, 5,000 bushels. A new type of minicontract is now available through some brokerage firms for just 1,000 bushels of grain, reducing the cash requirement and the risk. For gold, a contract is for 100 ounces.

Covering a short. Buying back a contract to sell, preferably at a lower price, but often not.

Day order. An order that will expire if not executed that business day.

Going long. Buying, in hopes the price will rise.

Going short. Selling a commodity you don't own, in hopes the price will fall.

Grain complex. A group of commodities, including wheat, corn, oats, and soybean products, that tend to be related in their price movement.

GTC. Good Till Cancelled: an order that stays in effect until the stated price is hit.

Limit order. An order to buy or sell at a set figure.

Limit move. The maximum amount an exchange allows a commodity to move up or down in one day, supposed to prevent huge losses by panic selling or buying. But it also locks traders in, so they may have to suffer through several days stuck in their positions, losing heavily each day.

Liquidating. Buying or selling enough to close out a long or short position.

Market order. An order to buy or sell at the current price.

Meat complex. Cattle, hogs, pork bellies, and iced broiling chickens, which generally show some relationship in their prices. Whenever one gets too costly, buyers start bidding for a substitute.

MOC. An order to buy or sell at the price at day's end: Market On Close.

MOO. Not just applicable to cattle; means Market On Opening.

Soybean complex. A group of three commodities that usually move similarly—soybeans, soybean oil, and soybean meal.

Split opening (or close). Prices of many commodities move so quickly that the opening or closing price covers a range of several points—you have to accept anything within that range.

Spread. Buying one contract and selling another, usually in the expectation that the gap between the two prices will change in your favor. The commonest spread involves buying a commodity for delivery in a certain month and selling for a different month. A spread can also involve two related commodities, such as cattle and hogs.

Stop. An order to buy if the price rises to a certain point or to sell if it drops to a certain point. It may be for the purpose of taking a profit or, if on the losing side, it may be a "defensive stop" to cut one's losses.

TLC. Not the Tender Loving Care given to your order, but Too Late to Cancel—an attempt to kill an order that reached the pit too late, so you're stuck with it.

18

Trading Money to Make Money

Some of the most fascinating speculations in the entire commodity field are in foreign currencies. *In the two successive economic periods that are now shaping up, I expect the excitement of currencies to be even greater than usual.* For each major government will be trying new ways to stimulate its economy, and the differences in their performances will inevitably show up as imbalances among their currencies. This will often cause futures contracts in foreign currencies to move strongly, and it can be very rewarding to those who take the right positions.

Let me explain at the outset that this should be done only after careful study and great attention to each separate deal. To go on feelings and hunches in this area is even more foolish than in the case of farm commodities or metals. Because you are actually speculating about the total position and performance of nations. And that involves many factors. Overlook one of them, and the currency you are expecting to fall may be on a sharp rise instead.

The currencies that are traded most on U.S. commodity exchanges are the Canadian dollar, the British pound, the German mark, the Swiss franc, and the Mexican peso. It is important to realize that trading these currencies also means *you are betting that the U.S. dollar will either rise or fall.* Sometimes, in fact, that may be the main thought. Anyone who believes that the dollar is about to weaken can express that view in speculative terms by selecting the foreign currency that looks the strongest and buying a futures contract in that currency.

If, for example, you *buy* Swiss francs for delivery six months from now, it is another way of saying that you expect the dollar to go *down* in terms of Swiss francs. You buy 125,000 Swiss francs which are worth, let's say, $50,000 today. Your hope is that the franc's rate will go from 40 cents to 50 cents, in which case those same 125,000 francs will be worth $62,500. On a margin of only $2,500 to $5,000, depending on your rating as a client, that can be a splendid return. Of course, leverage also works two ways: if the dollar fools you and goes up, meaning that the Swiss franc is worth less dollars, you may lose money rather fast.

Conversely, if you feel that the dollar has a major rise ahead, you look for the foreign currency that seems the weakest and *sell* a futures contract on it. If you decide to sell 20,000 pounds sterling when the rate is $1.80 to the pound, you are betting that $36,000 in U.S. money will move higher relative to the pound. If it does, if the pound indeed drops to $1.60, you cover that short position at a $4,000 profit—that is, you replace the 20,000 pounds you sold with 20,000 other pounds that you buy for only $32,000.

Trading Two Foreign Currencies

The only times that foreign currency trading is not really a speculation on the dollar's value is when you trade *two* foreign currencies, buying one and selling the other. In that case, you are dabbling in the European banker's game as he is often more involved in the "cross rates"—the rates between two European currencies—and not always thinking in terms of dollars.

Let's imagine that you hear England is about to make a big economic comeback that will pull its performance up closer to that of Germany. You decide to bet that this will result in a rise for the pound sterling vis-à-vis the German mark. You buy a contract for pounds and sell one for marks. It doesn't mean that marks are necessarily going to go down in relation to the U.S. dollar. You only care that they should go down in relation to the pound. You will almost certainly end up making money on one contract and losing on the other; it matters only that the gain on one exceeds the loss on the other.

It may be, for instance, that the deutschemark contract you sold with the mark at 42 cents—$52,500—can be repurchased with the mark at 38 cents—$47,500. Then even if the British pound loses a little ground in relation to the dollar and you sell your contract at a $1,000 loss, you still net $4,000 less commissions. In other words, both foreign currencies fell relative to the U.S. dollar, but you were right to believe that the pound was the stronger of the two and its fall was less. If your assessment had been wrong, you might have made some money on a rise in the British pound but wound up with a net loss because the German mark proved unexpectedly strong, rose to 46 cents, and caused you a $5,000 loss in covering your short position.

The Preferred Method

Here again, as in the more tangible commodities discussed in the last chapter, you can be either a *fundamental* trader or a *technical* trader. If you decide to rely on technical indexes, the chances are that your broker has figures at least as good as any that you are apt to calculate for yourself. In some offices, a running index on each currency is kept updated on the quotation machine that each broker uses. An expert in the home office does the daily work and indicates buy and sell points for each currency. At the punch of a button, your broker can tell you the indicated price for "going long Deutschemarks" or "going short British pounds."

The principle is about the same as it is for using an index to trade corn or cattle. You buy the foreign currency whenever the index of closing prices moves up to a certain point or sell it when that index drops to a certain level. It is the way that I suggest trading currencies because the numbers in that index embody the daily price performance that records the buying and selling convictions of all the big and sophisticated speculators in the major capitals of the world. People at trading desks in Chase Manhattan, Citibank, and many other giant American banks, in scores of financial institutions, in London, Zurich, Paris, Tokyo, and so on, and the traders in government central banks around the world: Their actions in multimillion dollar deals are reflected in the one rate you see on a broker's quotation screen. That means you get the benefit of their research and experience just by letting this one price index point the way.

THE FUNDAMENTAL BASIS

Despite all this convenience, it will be useful for you to know how to go about trading currencies on a fundamental basis. The factors that determine how high or low one type of money will move in relation to another are parts of the huge machine that is the international monetary system. And since it helps determine every other price in the world, an investor who has knowledge of its workings will find it easier to understand what is happening to his stocks, savings, or commodities. So let's suppose that you have decided to try trading foreign currencies on the basis of the fundamentals, and see what you have to look for:

Start by comparing the prosperity of each nation. A country in the midst of a boom is probably going to have a stronger currency than one that is in recession, although not for the straightforward reason you might expect. In fact, there are times when the boom itself and the outpouring of money to buy fuel and other imported goods can weaken the currency of a country. When you speculate, however, you think not so much about where the currency *is*, but where it is *going*. Modern economic methods call for a nation's monetary authorities to try to dampen a boom in order to curb inflation. Meanwhile, the officials of another country that is having a recession will feel that they should try to stimulate business. The mechanism that both will use is interest rates.

The boomy country will raise its rates to slow down business; the depressed nation will lower its rates to encourage business. Big money that is trying to earn the maximum return will tend to flow wherever rates are the highest. The controller of a company doing business in Europe will move cash from Germany to England if he sees the English rate move higher than the German one. Thousands of money managers will act in this same way. So you would be on the right side if you had decided to buy pounds and sell marks, because this shift of capital will make the pound worth more.

Or you might have done only half of that deal—let's say selling marks at a moment when it became obvious that the German government was about to ease its tough anti-inflation program and try to stimulate business by lowering interest rates. It might seem odd to be selling the currency of a nation that was moving toward a business surge. But your chief thought would be that a lower rate of return on German marks was very likely to make big holders of money move their funds out of Germany. Wherever they might move them, the mark would be apt to fall in relation to the U.S. dollar. So the marks you sold could later be repurchased for fewer dollars. A profitable trade.

What Affects a Currency?

This is highly simplistic. I start with it because interest rate differentials among nations are by far the greatest single factor that determines exchange rates. But some of the other ingredients can sometimes be strong enough to overcome this powerful fact. The ones I regard as paramount are: The rate and direction of inflation, the level of productivity, the balance of payments outlook, the labor situation, and the political stability of the nation.

Inflation is the best-known factor. Look again, for example, at a situation where Germany has decided to spur business expansion by easing interest rates. And let's say that Germany has only 3½% inflation at that time. Not very many money managers would rush to pull their money out of Germany just because it was going to earn a little less interest, because even if inflation went up by 1% or so, their cash would lose less buying power than it would in most other places. If they found another country with such low inflation and yet with higher interest rates, they might eventually move; but the jump would not be as hasty as it would be to get out of a currency suffering from double-digit inflation.

"**Real rate of interest,**" as economists call the decisive number, means the apparent rate minus the rate of inflation. If you have your cash in pounds sterling and are earning 18% interest when England's inflation rate is 14%, you only gain 4% in spending power at year's end (and even less if you are taxed on the 18% earnings). If you earn 11% interest in Germany when the inflation rate is 3½%, you have 7½% of real gain left. You can afford to wait and see whether a 1% drop in interest rate and the possible rise in inflation is going to push your "real rate of interest" low enough to warrant switching into another currency.

Productivity of a nation's workers can also play a part in how the currency traders treat its money. Productivity is a statistic that goes one step deeper than inflation. It is one of the foundations on which the country's price structure is based. A national workforce that turns out more goods per man-hour can afford to pay out higher wages and other costs and still price its products competitively. Here again, England has rated low for years. Germany and Japan have been near the top. An interest-rate drop that would cause the pound to plunge would do very little to the mark or yen, because traders would feel it was unlikely that inflation in such productive countries would rise to the point of making the *real* rate of interest unattractive.

The balance of trade—how much a country takes in from selling its goods and services to others compared with how much it pays out for foreign products—has a big role in a currency's outlook because if it goes into red ink, too much of the nation's money is flowing out and causing a glut of it. But this simple trade balance is less important than the balance of *payments,* which includes cash that flows in or out for investment purposes. A nation that takes in large amounts of investment capital from abroad may show a big surplus in international payments, even if it has a deficit in the straight exchange of goods. And such a surplus means that it is sucking in currency, rather than letting it flow out. This is a plus factor for its exchange rate. It doesn't mean that the rate can't fall, but it is unlikely to fall far as long as the outlook for the future payments balance remains positive.

The country's labor situation, much like its productivity, helps to foretell where its inflation rate is headed. If there is nearly full employment and if there are also lots of strike threats, very analytical traders will assume that large wage increases are likely and that they will eventually lead to higher inflation. So, long before that time comes they will start to back away from the currency, selling out their positions before the drop becomes too widespread. A country with high unemployment is generally thought to have a lower inflation outlook, because there are technical formulas indicating that each percentage point in the unemployment figure has a certain lowering effect on the inflation rate. This is far from proved, but it has enough acceptance to affect exchange rates a little. Strike threats and labor unrest, however, are much more influential. They tend to depress a currency, partly because markets always dislike uncertainty and partly because they point to higher wages, lower productivity, more inflation—all the adverse factors listed above rolled into one.

Finally, the political climate of a country is very significant in affecting its exchange rate. A stable government may be more or less taken for granted in most major nations and may not be a big plus in the currency markets. But *instability,* such as the entry of an untested socialist government into power in France, the threatened break-up of the ruling Social Democrat Party in Germany, or the collapse of still another Italian cabinet, is a big depressant. People who control large sums do not want to bet them merely on the hope that policies will be consistent and agreeable. Just the knowledge that change *could* come is enough to make a currency slide.

Keeping Posted

Like so many things that seem enormously complex, the facts that govern the outlook for a nation's currency are much less formidable once they are listed. Note that I have given only six items—five arithmetical and one psychological. If you wonder how anyone can keep being informed on them, it is also reasonably simple. *The Wall Street Journal* gives a good deal of this information about major countries. *The Journal of Commerce* carries more details. London's *Economist* touches on the affairs of many more countries and presents them in very readable form. And *The Financial Times,* originating in London and available here in a U.S. edition, is the fullest source of all for anyone who really wants to keep up with these trend-setting figures for the world's leading countries.

THE TECHNICAL WAY

While asserting that a sophisticated investor who has the time and inclination can definitely act as his own expert and decide which way the fundamental forces are likely to move a currency, *I strongly recommend that an index system be used instead.* A personal example may help explain why:

I, of course, follow all these factors within each country regularly, and have access to confidential sources that alert me to trends well ahead of the time when they appear in the press. In the great majority of cases, my assessment of which way a currency will move has been correct. Yet if I had backed one of my judgments with cash in the currency futures market I would have fared badly.

Late in 1979, I decided that the German economy was in for trouble and that the Deutschemark would surely be affected adversely in the coming year. All through 1980 I waited for the drop to come. But it didn't really set in until 1981. The reward for being too foresighted in the futures market is just about as painful as being wrong.

If I had shorted Deutschemarks early in 1980, I would have been a big loser, and no amount of belated satisfaction would have restored the lost money. On the other hand, an index system would have floundered rather inconclusively for quite a while, making some gains when the mark moved upward against my expectations, taking small losses in periods of fluctuation, then finally moving to the very lucrative short side when the German currency began to fall in earnest.

Knowing how to assess the fundamental outlook is valuable,

for it helps you to understand the cross-currents of world business. And this firmer knowledge can alert you to the time when the new crisis stage is approaching—the time when market jumpiness will make it wise to take your profits in a number of investments and concentrate on safety. But here, as in general commodity trading, you are urged to evaluate your currency trading decisions on the basis of the index approaches that are available to you. Even though you pass up part of the potential profits by waiting for some rise before you buy and for some decline before you sell, there will be plenty of reward when you do hit a good trend.

TRADING CURRENCIES
FOR THE CAUTIOUS BUSINESSMAN

Apart from personal speculation in currencies, if you are in a business that buys, sells, or gets royalties from abroad, you should give careful consideration to foreign currency trading as a way to hedge against loss. In that case, it becomes a form of insurance, a way to *cut* risk. Note this well, for some very sophisticated businessmen find it hard to grasp the point.

I was shocked to hear the Controller of one of New York's largest retail chains say, "We thought about doing some hedging in the financial futures market in case the dollar should fall. But I reminded the board that we are merchandisers, not money traders, and they decided to stay out of such things." He said it as if they had made a cautious decision. The fact is they had neglected a very prudent step just because it was new to them. A riverboat gambler would shudder at the risk they were taking—being obligated for several million dollars worth of foreign merchandise that would have cost them 10% to 15% more in case of a sudden dollar drop.

A few thousand dollars—free of any other risk—would have protected them totally. By buying futures contracts on the foreign currencies they expect to owe to suppliers abroad, at a commission cost of $70 or $80 on each one, they could insure against all exchange-rate losses.

19

Getting Income from Your Gold and Silver

You can add comfort and extra luxuries to your life, and especially to your retirement, by "living on your precious metals" and still having them there as investments. Does that sound like eating your cake and having it too? No, it can really be done. You can either arrange this on your own, or let an institution do the job for you. Either way, you should know the principle so that you do not entrust your financial future to any plan that you do not understand.

- Briefly stated, the principle is to hold a substantial amount of gold or silver and sell a predetermined quantity of it at certain fixed dates each year.

Actually this is the reverse of the gradual accumulation process. I have described how you can "average in" to a long-term asset by making regular purchases on a highly disciplined basis. In the case of an anti-inflation metal, that means you will usually be paying more and more on successive purchases. The same principle allows you to sell off parts of your holdings over a remarkably long period of time, get a great deal of spendable cash, and still have quite a lot left.

Sales can be made monthly, quarterly, or once or twice a year. I suggest quarterly sales because they will give you something quite close to the year's average price. Whatever sales dates you choose in advance, you *must* adhere to them strictly and never delay in the hope of getting a better price.

This would turn a conservative program into another form of speculation.

Examples of the results tend to be dramatized because the soaring precious metals prices of the last decade made everything go especially well. There is no way to avoid this, because going back to the time when prices were artificially depressed by government action would be equally unrepresentative. So, one striking example of the 1970–1979 decade and a shorter, and somewhat steadier, period are used to illustrate that the principle is sound even apart from statistical distortions.

As the adjoining graph illustrates, a one-time purchase of $100,000 worth of gold in 1970 was sold off at the rate of 10% of the *remaining* gold each year. Note that the gold never becomes exhausted in this way because the sale is always just 10% of what remains. That leaves 90% after the first year, 81% after the second year, 73% after the third year, and so on. By the end of 1979, a total of $202,000 in income would have been received; and 968 ounces of gold were still left—worth $297,000 at the average gold price that prevailed throughout the year 1979. (Actually worth $506,000 at December 31, 1979 when the price had jumped to $523 per ounce.)

Taking a much less favorable starting point, we still get an astonishing result: $100,000 invested in gold in 1975, just before a sharp price drop and a three-year lull, would have yielded $62,180 in income if sold off on the same 10%-per-year basis over the six years through 1981. And . . . there would have been 267 ounces of gold left on hand at that point—worth $120,150.

Incidentally, either silver or platinum would have given similar results during any of these periods, with silver yielding an even greater return on the original investment but with a less consistent yearly income.

When Not to Start

The absolutely critical rule is not to start any such plan at a historic high point in the price performance of the metal. You

GOLDPLAN^{SM}
Gold Income Plan

This graph shows the income created from a $100,000 purchase of gold (2,277.78 ozt.) in 1970. Each quarter thereafter 10 percent of the remaining ounces were sold for dollars.

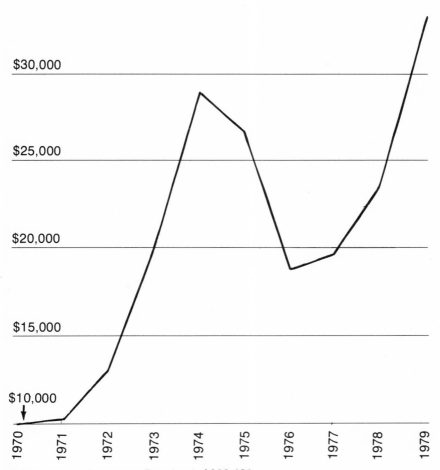

Total Income Payments Received: **$202,429**

Total Ounces Sold: **1,809.20ozt**

Total Ounces Remaining At Average 1979 Gold Price: **$297,354**

Value of Ounces Remaining As Of December 31, 1979 At $523/ozt: **$506,567**

Calculations based on average monthly gold price in U.S. dollars: numbers rounded cannot always know what a price pattern will look like later, can never be sure that a high price will not go higher. BUT you can always know whether or not the metal is already at levels that it has not ever seen before, or at least not in recent history. For instance, you may think that the first dramatic example given could only have been recorded by starting at a time when gold was around $40 an ounce. That made the example more startling, of course. But anyone who realized in 1976 that gold had fallen to little more than half of its $200 high point of 1974 could have begun the plan at that point and done remarkably well with it.

The key fact is, of course, that these materials move with inflation. Their performance is even more astonishing when seen in that light because they provide an assurance of buying power, rather than just numerical dollars. If, for example, there were a long stagnant period in the economy, or an actual deflation, the governments of the world would be trying hard to stimulate business. Their moves would drive up the value of precious metals.

Historically and actually, gold has been as good an anti-DEFLATION as anti-INFLATION hedge. So even while getting lower income figures for each 10% sale, you would be receiving more power to buy goods in a deflationary period. Houses, cars, trips, appliances, food—whatever you might want—would be purchasable at lower prices. If the income for this plan were portrayed in goods, rather than dollar figures, it would look about equally good, regardless of the times we were living through.

It is my opinion, although disputed by some precious metals enthusiasts, that a plan of this kind should be only a part of your financial or retirement program. The income might serve as well as any other possible investment; it might even, as in the case of the 1970's, make a person wealthy while he had been merely trying to assure a comfortable income. But here again, as in every other technique I propose in this book, I like to spread a safety net. Things that have never happened before can happen for the first time. Any plan for future income should put no more than a third of its emphasis on this kind of program.

A Steady Income Booster

Just look at how this can brighten your outlook, as illustrated by the case history of a retiree. This person had spent his last four working years accumulating gold and silver in quarterly purchases, averaging his cost along the lines I suggested earlier. On retirement, he had accumulated $30,000 worth of these precious metals and $20,000 worth of gold stocks. At that point, he began to sell 10% of his precious metals each year. A period of high inflation followed, and he found himself taking in far more money than he had expected because this portion of his investments was selling for sums that greatly outstripped the Consumer Price Index. His pension was augmented by about $6,000 yearly income from the sale of coins and $2,000 more dividends on gold shares. And he has a considerable amount of gold and silver still in reserve for the time when inflation worsens.

There is, as mentioned earlier, a Swiss company that operates this type of plan—buys gold for your account and sells it for you at whatever preset periods you stipulate. It has a variety of plans for acquiring the metal, in a lump sum or gradually; and for selling it off according to your needs. Among the advantages are that it stores the gold for you, and that it is housed in Switzerland, a country that has never confiscated gold. The firm is called Goldplan A.G., member of the Assurex group of companies. Exact details can be obtained by writing to Goldplan AG, Volkmarstrasse 10, P.O. Box 209, 8033 Zurich, Switzerland.

Weigh the pros and cons carefully before you decide whether to operate a plan of this kind on your own or to entrust it to an institution. Persons who are fairly adept at calculating figures, and who feel they have the self-discipline to keep to a prearranged plan regardless of sudden price shifts or news headlines may get along perfectly well without the outside help. There may be a little saving of costs in this way. On the other hand, the Goldplan people are able to more than pay for their cost of serving you because they are buying and selling gold in bulk quantities.

Using the Gold-Silver Relationship

If you are already accustomed to owning precious metals, you may want to know about more advanced techniques that can add to your profit potential. A number of possibilities are opened up by realizing that the relative prices of gold and silver periodically get out of line with each other and then return to the normal ratio of between 30 to 1 and 35 to 1. Some analysts insist that this ratio will keep moving higher and higher in favor of gold; in other words, to an average of 38 to 1, then 40 to 1, and so on. This is by no means certain, in my opinion. Even if it turns out to be so, it will take quite a few years to change appreciably. Between each upward jog in the ratio, the move back in the general direction of what is called normal will afford you a considerable chance to benefit.

In the simplest instance, there are times when you can buy silver as a substitute for investing in gold—relying on the fact that the two metals will run along roughly similar paths. One reason for doing this is if you want to make many very small purchases at regular intervals. Even a few gold coins add up to a substantial amount. But at a time when a single Kruger-rand is selling for $500, ten silver quarters would cost only $30 to $35.

THE BARGAIN OF THE MOMENT

Then there are times when silver is more attractive than gold for the bigger investor. Let's suppose that you have nothing whatever committed to precious metals. You are considering a purchase of $10,000 worth of gold coins in order to have the anti-inflation hedge. You notice that the price of gold is 46 times the price of silver (as it actually is while I write this). You know it means that silver is cheaper than it should be in relation to gold. The relationship *could* move in the wrong direction, of course, based on recurrent rumors that the Hunts or the U.S. government are about to drop silver onto the market.

As I have pointed out before, you can never be sure that the price of any item will go where "it ought to be." But you should certainly conclude that the odds favor the historical relationship of two items rather than a total departure from it. So you assume that whether silver goes up or down, it is likely to do better than gold in the near future. For the moment, then, buying silver is an advantageous way to get in on the gold price. You invest your $10,000 in a bag of silver coins rather than in gold.

If, in due course, the price ratio of the two metals does move to 33 to 1, you are better off—whether that change comes about during a rise or a fall in the precious metals market. If it happens because both metals move up, your bag of coins may be worth $15,000 to $16,000. If the metals fall instead, the silver will have fallen less than gold in that same period. So your $10,000 may be temporarily reduced to $9,000; but gold would have fallen to $7,000 in that same time. The important thing is that silver purchased at such a point will be worth more than the gold you would otherwise have bought.

WHEN GOLD IS CHEAPER THAN SILVER

Continuing a bit further, let us say that another big silver run-up swings the ratio in the opposite direction—to only 25 to 1. By then, your silver bag is worth $5,000 more than the same investment in gold would have been. And noticing that silver is now *overpriced* relative to gold, you sell your silver and put that cash into gold coins.

The procedure is very simple. You just call the dealer you bought the silver from, and ask, "How much are you paying for a bag of silver coins today?" When he names the price, you ask, "How many Krugerrands (or Maple Leafs) can I buy for that much money?" If the answer satisfies you, you say, "It's a deal. I'll sell you the silver and buy that many gold coins." By the time the old 33 to 1 ratio shows up again, you have gained another $1,500 on the trade. Again, this is true regardless of whether the metals rise or fall. Just because this time the gold you bought outperformed the silver you sold.

An experienced investor can find repeated opportunities to apply the same principle in a variety of ways. Bear in mind that gold has, on recent occasions, spurted to 50 times the cost of silver, and the cheaper metal has, during its own price flurries, narrowed the gap to as low as 18 to 1. Anyone who is accustomed to trading on the commodity futures market could have *sold silver short* when it was up to $1/18$ the price of gold and *bought gold* at the same moment.

What? Sell silver when it was $45 an ounce and possibly headed much higher? Yes, and quite safely too, because you have been buying gold at $810 an ounce. If that upward thrust in all precious metals had continued, gold would finally have outperformed silver in order to get back to the 33 to 1 ratio. You would have made enough on the gold contract to outweigh the loss on the silver.

As it was, both metals fell. And when gold got down to $400, you would have lost more than half of your investment in it. But . . . silver had fallen to $8.50 per ounce by then—an 80% gain to more than make up for your 50% loss in gold. Assuming that you had bought three gold contracts and sold one silver contract (that proportion being necessary in order to make the dollar amounts equal on either side), you would have lost about $122,000 on gold and gained some $180,000 on silver—a net gain of $58,000. This is an idealized figure, and not wholly realistic, since the jagged ups and downs of commodity trading would probably have induced you to close out the deal before the two metals fell that much. But the principle is absolutely valid, and you can see how great an opportunity it presents for those who are alert and patient.

Special Use of Mining Stocks

There are other ways to "own" silver and even to use the arbitrage principle without actually buying the metal or trading in the futures market. Persons who feel uncomfortable with commodity trading can accomplish some of the same effect with common stocks; in this case, gold-mining and silver-mining stocks. If the ratio of gold to silver indicates that silver is set to outperform gold for a while, you would probably gain by buying a leading silver stock, such as Sunshine Mining or Hecla Mining, and selling short a gold stock like ASA Ltd. Or if short selling does not appeal to you, you could buy a "put" option on the ASA stock, which would mean that

you gain if that stock falls. Then if you have correctly estimated that silver will do better than gold, you should come
out with a net gain, because the action of these stocks tends to
follow the prices of the metals themselves.

A Special Way to Trade Commodities Risk-Free

There is a form of commodity trading that can be done entirely without risk if you already own some gold or silver. This
is not to say that you are certain to make profits, only that you
can be sure of not losing if you stick to the discipline of the
program. That means you enjoy the chance of gain without
the usual risk of being hurt.

It works this way: Say you own some gold coins, or silver
coins, valued at $50,000. Your plan is to hold them as insur-
ance against the higher inflation that is coming. But you are
not averse to using part of them as a pledge against possible
reverses in the futures market. You keep a careful index of
price movements of both gold and silver futures on the exchanges, along the lines indicated in the chapter on commodity trading. And you wait for the index to give a *sell* signal.

(If your system gives a signal to buy either of these metals,
ignore it. You already own them, and any new purchase
would be a duplication. Buying in the futures market, although it starts as only a paper transaction, is the same as
buying the metal. It puts you in the position of wishing for a
rising price, just as purchase of the actual metal does.)

Whenever your system, or the one kept by your broker or
fund manager, signals that it is time to sell either gold or
silver, go ahead with the sale of one contract for a month well
in the future. This amount—100 ounces of gold or 5,000
ounces in the case of silver—will be covered by the actual
gold you own. The system is predicting that precious metals
are going to fall for a while. If this is correct, you may be able
to "cover" your short position in futures at a price five or six
thousand dollars lower than your sale figure.

You still own your coins. They are worth less for the moment, but of course they will bounce back some months
hence. The only difference is that instead of seeing your coins

go down and up in value without taking part in either move, you have pocketed a gain of several thousand dollars.

Suppose the short sale doesn't work out well. The metal price goes up instead. You lose on the futures contract. But you don't pay for the loss in cash, you sell enough of your coins to pay for the loss. Meanwhile, the remaining coins in your bank vault have gone up in value, so your only real regret is that you did not make the hoped-for cash profit. Not that time around. But you can try it the next time your system signals a short sale. Historical experience shows that you will gain about 50% of the time. But since any futures trading system you select should have automatic stops that hold your losses to about a third the size of your gains, you emerge with a trading profit at the end of any given period.

Two Precautions

Two more points must be emphasized in order to be certain of maximum safety:

First, since your store of coins will diminish each time you have a trading loss and sell some to cover it, it is wise to replenish exactly that *number* of coins (number, not current value) whenever a falling price makes that favorable.

To give an example of how this might work, suppose you lost $2,000 after sales of a silver futures contract against you. You sell 500 quarters—$150 face value of silver coins, which yields enough to pay for your loss. You do not replenish these coins for the moment, but just take a tax loss on the bad trade and wait for the next time your system gives a sell signal.

This time the trade goes in your favor, silver falls in price, and you gain $4,800 before the trend turns upward again. At that point, you use part of the new cash to repurchase 500 quarters—$150 face value of silver coins in order to have your original hoard back. Since the premium on coins tends to shrink when prices are down, these cost only $1,600 now. So you have a net gain of $3,200 and all your original coins are back in the vault.

Second, do not let your store of precious metals fall below a certain minimum level. The ideal way to do this trading is to back the contracts with coins that are separate from your inflation-hedge supply, although this may not be practical for many persons. If your total investment capital is $200,000, and your precious metals—as suggested earlier—are about 20% of that, you have $40,000 in gold and silver. It may not be practical to have another $40,000 in the same kind of assets for this other purpose. There are too many attractive things to do with your capital. So you do use the basic $40,000 to back your futures trades.

Since nothing is impossible and a succession of unfortunate trades could reduce your supply of coins lower and lower, be sure to draw the line at some point and stop this kind of trading any time your remaining coins are down to only 15% of your total asset value. The risk of this coming about is actually quite small; remember that it would happen only if time after time your short sales were ruined by a surge in the metal price. That would mean a much higher price level was developing, so you would have had to sell very few coins to meet the trading losses. And your remaining coins would have an enhanced dollar value.

Trading against your own gold and silver in this way is not to everyone's liking. It takes more careful watching of the markets than many persons want to do. I have found that most techniques involving simultaneous buying and selling or any other multifaceted form of trade tend to worry anyone who has not tried them. It is strange how often this last thought is really all that stands in the way. I know farmers who have made very intricate arrangements with cooperatives and banks for the advance sale of their crops, yet who say, "That's way over my head!" if confronted with a much simpler commodity or option deal that is new to them.

I do not emphasize this in order to urge you to trade against your precious metals. It is not that big an issue. What I do urge is that you study this and every other technique with the assurance that it is far simpler than it appears once the first step is taken.

20

The Next Great Stars—The More-Than-Precious Minerals

With inflation set to soar in the next few years, and with the world political situation so delicate, I want you to be aware of a subject that you might not care about in more tranquil times:

There are 36 metals and minerals that our government regards as *critical* to the continued operation of our industry. In many of those cases, we depend on foreign sources for more than half of our supply, including such a metal as cobalt. Every jet engine needs over 900 pounds of it—and 97% of what we use comes from abroad. Also included in the list is the much more exotic germanium, which sounds obscure, but without it there can be no lasers or semiconductors. Similarly, *important parts of our advanced technology would be wiped out* if we lacked cadmium, indium, rhodium, or selenium.

These materials are used in relatively small quantities, compared with the large amounts of copper, lead, aluminum, nickel, and tin that industry processes. But they have the ability to alter the strength, melting point, and other properties of the major metals. So without them, making certain alloys is impossible. And most of these materials come from countries that are caught up in political and racial instability.

Risk of a Cut-Off

As long ago as 1954, a Senate Subcommittee on Minerals, Materials and Fuels reported that the national security was in danger of too much reliance on foreign sources. Nothing was done then; and very little has been done since. The whole industrial world remains vulnerable to a sudden cut-off that could rival the fuel shortage in seriousness.

Of the 23 vital minerals that the United States gets mostly from abroad, there are eight cases where almost *all* of the supply comes from places like Zambia, Zaire, and Zimbabwe, where an upheaval or a deliberate ploy might produce a momentous stoppage. And . . . from the Soviet Union. It would be astonishing if the Soviets did not, at some point, create a squeeze for us on materials that they control directly or through their influence on some Third World nations. After all, the United States deliberately uses the export of grains or high technology as an instrument of international policy. When we want to discourage the Kremlin from moving into a neighbor country, we order an embargo on shipments of wheat or instruct our computer companies to deny the Soviets their latest information. Why shouldn't the Russians use their own advantages in the same way?

They have been preparing for such an eventuality for decades. The pattern of their interest in diverse parts of the world indicates heavy emphasis on areas that have vital materials and those that could potentially interrupt international transport.

The U.S. public, quite naturally, fails to get excited about such a possibility, and so fails to prod its elected leaders on it. Who knows or cares what chromite or raw cobalt or manganese looks like? These will remain just names until they suddenly become front-page headlines. Too late for most citizens to do anything but read. But a very few who take the trouble to think about these things in advance will reap enormous rewards.

Worsening Trend

A study for the National Academy of Sciences recently concluded: "The fact that the United States is strategically more vulnerable to a long-term chromium embargo than to an embargo of any other natural resource, including petroleum, has not been recognized." We get about 90% of our chromite from overseas sources—much of it from the U.S.S.R. We are near that point in cobalt, manganese, and the platinum group. Without those minerals, there can be no stainless steel, no armor plate, no jet engines, no batteries. We have a strategic stockpile, but it holds only a small fraction of the projected goals. There are also less-known minerals which, in very small quantities, could strangle us even more neatly. Without tantalum, for example, certain cutting tools are not efficient.

Moreover, we don't have to look to such exotic materials to find causes of strategic concern. Because the U.S. has to think beyond its own borders—to the situations of its chief allies and trading partners. Germany, for example, depends on outside sources for 100% of its bauxite, 100% of its copper, 82% of its lead, and 64% of its zinc. Japan has almost total dependency on other nations for nearly all its basic materials.

While many countries simply have no alternative but to keep importing and pray, the United States could do a lot more to develop its own resources, especially in the untapped mineral richness of Alaska. But environmental considerations will stand in the way. That plus the day-to-day economics that makes it so much more desirable to keep buying from low-cost sources abroad rather than invest huge sums in developing our own.

The trend continued, even after the 1954 report: We depended on foreign sources for 50% or more of our needs in only four strategic minerals then; that figure has, of course, worsened greatly. At that time, we had a trade surplus in minerals; we sold more than we imported. Today, however, we have a deficit of many billions of dollars in that area.

The Potential for Gains

What happens when an important mineral suddenly becomes scarce? You don't have to rely on hunches to get a good idea. The U.S.S.R. put an embargo on chromite exports to the United States during the Korean War. Washington had to use strict price controls; but even in those days when American primacy in many foreign areas and supply lines was in far less jeopardy than today, nothing prevented a big escalation of price and the growth of black markets. In 1978, Zaire's Shaba Province was invaded briefly by forces from nearby Angola. That is the region that produces a large part of the world's cobalt. And cobalt prices jumped from $6.40 to $50 a pound on the spot market. (The Soviets, incidentally, had bought up all the cobalt they could find on the world markets and sold it to the West at massive prices.)

What can you do about all this? Needlessly to say such a situation opens up great possibilities for the alert speculator. There are two different ways of tapping the important money-making opportunities in the strategic metals and minerals: Either buying and holding the materials themselves. Or choosing foreign stocks that would benefit from price increases in these metals.

Buying Australian Mining Stocks

The easiest way to get in on the potential scarcity of these items is by the routine process of buying foreign stocks. Australia is the one friendly and stable nation capable of delivering large amounts of various strategic materials. Many major brokerage firms, such as Drexel Burnham Lambert, E.F. Hutton, and Dean Witter Reynolds, have research departments that go into the subject thoroughly. They can tell you about Australian common stocks that are tied to these resources.

In these days when energy costs have so much to do with ability to compete in the world, you can imagine the continuing and growing advantages that Australian metals producers will have on the basis of this comparison: Electric energy costs about 3.8 cents per kilowatt hour in the United States and only 2 cents in Australia.

The giant of the Australian metals and minerals field is Broken Hill Proprietary, a major stock whose only drawback is that the sheer size of the company and its holdings prevent it from spurting upward on any single development. New finds or market changes that might triple the value of a lesser company only nudge BHP upward by a point or two. But its steady growth will add up to a large gain over the years—as an investment, not a speculation.

Other important Australian firms in this field include Western Mining Corporation, which is closely linked to our own aluminum giant, ALCOA; and Colonial Sugar Refining Co., which, despite its name, is highly diversified into the metals and minerals field.

On the other hand, the brokers who study Australian stocks carefully can also tell you about companies that are just developing from the exploratory to the production stage. Some of these sell for only a few dollars a share. Obviously they involve the higher speculative risk that goes with newness, but their potential for multiplying in value is very exciting.

Buying Minerals

The more direct way is to buy and hold the materials themselves. The minimum qualifications are: Enough capital to diversify into a good many different areas. Enough time to study the uses and availability of each material. Enough patience to hold a commitment until it really ripens.

For those who are able to put a part of their cash into this type of deal, there is an element of the "perfect investment." Perfect in the sense that whatever happens is likely to favor you. Bear in mind our guiding principle that a smooth-running world benefits the investor and a world of crises benefits the speculator. If—against my expectations—the world goes smoothly, it will also be a growing world with greater industrial activity because a growing population requires increased production to maintain equilibrium. This will automatically raise the demand for and the prices of strategic materials. Since their supply is limited, any greater demand has to be reflected in higher prices. But if—as I expect by mid-decade—the world goes into spasms of crisis, the prices of these materials will jump even further and faster.

It is the huge jumps linked to crises that bring the greatest rewards. But few persons are in a position to keep large amounts of money tied up while waiting for the moment of crisis to occur. So one technique that plants a foot in each of these timing areas is to invest in quantities of strategic materials that are divisible. In other words, to buy at least ten tons of antimony, so that a five-ton lot could be sold if, some months later, an upsurge in prices should bring say a 35% profit. Then to hold the remaining five tons until a moment of much greater gain, which could be fixed either to a specific political happening, or to the achievement of a certain price objective. I favor the latter. Being overly greedy usually results in seeing paper profits dwindle and having to accept something less. Study enough to know what average level of gains on capital are expectable. Then set a selling figure a little below that.

Trading these vital metals and minerals is basically *speculation*, even when the material is held for a long time. As I have pointed out earlier, the speculator gains most when he bets correctly on a sudden turn that others have overlooked. Such a turn is virtually certain to bring on a crisis in strategic materials during the next few years and to plague the world spasmodically for the rest of the century.

The Steps in Trading

The ways to trade such minerals seem remote and difficult only until you look into them and get used to them. Then they will be no harder than buying gold coins or common stocks.

The fact that not many people engage in this kind of deal may pose a psychological barrier. You are not likely to have the feeling of moral support when hearing a colleague or a golfing companion say, "I bought 1,000 drums of ferrovanadium yesterday." But the principle is no different from buying 100 shares of General Electric stock. In either case, a phone call to a broker, then a check in payment are all that is needed.

The selection of a broker is of greatest importance. *There are some outright crooks in the field.* Even legitimate firms sometimes overcharge enormously because they have to deal through too many intermediaries. Some are known to charge 100% or more above true market prices. This can be avoided by patronizing only the outstanding companies that have set up special divisions to trade strategic metals. Bache and Company is one such firm. Another is Strategic Metals and Critical Materials, Inc., of New York City.

After you make a purchase through such a company, you get five documents:

- A confirmation of sale, showing quantity, minimum grade, price, and commission charge.
- A warehouse receipt issued by a warehouse that is approved by the LME (London Metals Exchange).
- A sampling certificate, showing that an inspector saw and weighed the material.
- An assayer's report, stating its purity.
- An insurance statement indicating Lloyds of London coverage.

The mechanics of the deal, in other words, are not really difficult. The problem is knowing what and when to buy. If you are prepared to hold on indefinitely, you will eventually profit from any of these critical materials. Even the course of inflation and normal expansion of world industrial needs would ensure this, not to mention the abnormalities that are ahead of us. But holding drums of metal that pay no dividends—in fact, that actually *cost* money to store and insure—can become difficult if it goes on too long. So it is highly desirable to give great care to the matter of timing.

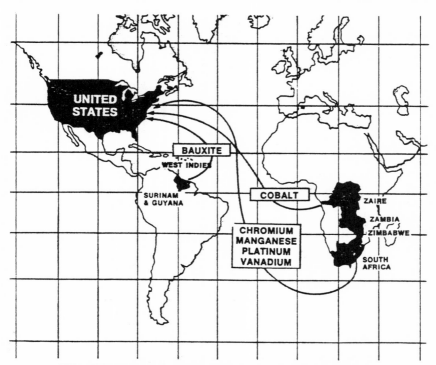

THE POTENTIAL STRATEGIC MINERALS CRISIS

The New York Times or *The Wall Street Journal* can keep you sufficiently informed on the political situations in the African continent and on the movements of Soviet-leaning rebels in countries that have some of these critical materials or control their flow to the outside world. And any regular reader of the financial pages can become aware of the times when the economic cycle tends to depress the prices of these raw materials. That is when the pros like to accumulate anything— when it is relatively plentiful and prices are somewhat soft.

Some Recommended Metals

James Sinclair, one of the leading authorities on world materials prices, has included the following recommendations in his list of minerals that can usually be purchased and held in the expectation of substantial gains:

- Antimony, in five-ton lots of ingots, at 99.6% purity and maximum arsenic content of 0.25%, packed in wooden cases.
- Chromium, in lots of one metric ton, in the form of lumps of 99.0% minimum purity, packed in steel drums.
- Cobalt, in lots of 250 kilos in broken cathodes, 99.6% minimum purity, packed in steel drums.
- Germanium, in lots of 20 kilos, in ingots, 99.99% minimum purity, 50 ohm resistivity, in wooden boxes.
- Electromanganese, in 100-ton lots, as flakes of 99.95% minimum purity, in steel drums.
- Rhodium, in lots of 20 troy ounces of sponge, minimum purity 99.9%.
- Titanium, in lots of 500 kilos of irregular granules (sponge), of 99.6% typical purity, in drums.

21

Putting All This Together to Form Your Financial Strategy

I have described 12 types of investment or speculation that you can now draw from to form a financial plan of your own.

Most of these are simple to act on; in fact, you may be already involved in some of them. Nearly everyone is in stocks and bonds, directly or indirectly, because every pension fund has cash invested in these assets. What I do hope is that you now have more of a feel of what each one is like, that unfamiliarity will not prevent you from considering some addition to the techniques you use to increase your capital.

Now it is time to decide what combination of methods you will put together. Clearly, you cannot use all of the available techniques. What is needed is an overall strategy that combines several of these wealth-enhancing ideas in a way that is *safe and appropriate for you.*

Your choice of a plan has to be tailored to fit your income, tax bracket, career, and family situation. There is no point in owning tax-free municipal bonds if you are in a low tax bracket. There is no sense in planning to acquire gold coins every three months if you can hardly keep up with the financial needs of children in college. There is not the slightest excuse for trading commodities or strategic minerals if you are a retiree on a restricted income. These points may seem too obvious to mention, but they serve to emphasize the reverse side of each such constraining situation. For all three of those personal dilemmas do leave room for *some* attempt to make financial progress:

- The person whose tax bracket is low can invest without worrying whether too much of his gains will be taken by the government. He can, for instance, look into investments that pay the highest dividends, including money market funds, utilities, and gold shares.
- The parents who have little cash during their children's college years can look for something highly leveraged, where a small down payment has the potential to build up over the next few years. A small home that can be rented for enough monthly income to cover all charges is an example. For such a family, the risk of losing the down payment is much less than the possible rewards as the equity mounts over the years.
- The retiree who has to stay away from the most exotic speculations can augment his income with the high dividends from utilities stocks and the likelihood of capital gains in years to come.

As a general rule, your attitude toward cash should be one thing if you are in the retired category, and just the opposite if you have many working years ahead.

If you have built up substantial assets you should now be getting cash out of them at a rate that gives you as nearly as possible the living standard of your choice. This can even include placing a small mortgage on a fully paid-up home, or selling off small parts of stock or gold holdings to get more usable income. But it is best if the amounts can come from investments that yield more return without having to be sold, as shown in some of the sample plans below.

If you are at an early stage of your financial career you should be putting cash into investments that will build up valuable assets for the future. This may involve investing part of your salary for that purpose, or even incurring debt to buy property or stocks, as long as you can see the probability of paying it off in the normal course of things.

The Different Stages in Your Career

I have referred many times in this book to the youthful investor and to the retiree as a convenient way of illustrating typical situations. But it is not intended to compartmentalize individuals, and certainly not to impose limits on freedom of action.

There is no reason at all to close the door on creative investing when you are in your eighties, just because you are called a "retiree." If you happen to be wealthy or have a source of considerable income beyond your living needs, you should by all means use the guidelines suggested for aggressive investors. By the same reasoning, a young investor who is forced to live on a disability pension should follow the plans suggested for more cautious investors. The real distinction, not on the basis of age, is between those who will have more cash coming in steadily for some years to come and those whose chance of earning important new money has diminished.

If your circumstances or inclinations make it unlikely that you will be earning much more than your minimum needs from salaried work in the future, it is all the more vital to concentrate on ways of producing more income by way of the investment route. Do not be deceived by the thought, "I have enough to live on." What seems to be enough today is unlikely to remain so.

Sample Plans to Choose From

Here are some examples of balanced portfolios to give an idea of the many types of formulas that you can select—ranging from the cautious to the aggressive:

	PERCENTAGE OF TOTAL CAPITAL	SUITABLE IF
Blue chip stocks	15	You are a retired person in a
(bought below 10 times earnings)		low tax bracket, need more
Money market fund	25	income, and can afford very
Gold stocks	15	little risk.
Gold coins	10	
Utilities stocks	35	
Under-$20-per-share listed stocks	20	You want income and
Corporate bond fund	25	growth, and you are in a
Money market fund	35	low-to-medium tax bracket.
Silver coins	10	(Note that bond funds and
Gold stocks	10	money funds move counter
		to each other, so the two
		combined will pay a steady
		good return, regardless of
		interest-rate changes.)
Stock options	10	An alternate plan for income
Money market fund	60	and growth if you are in a
Gold stocks	15	low-to-moderate tax
Gold coins	15	bracket.
Stock options	5	You have a moderately
Short-term stock trading	10	good income, and are within
Money market fund	25	10 years of retirement. You
Silver coins	10	want some chance to
Gold coins	20	expand capital, but you are
Utilities stocks	30	also converting to the higher
		returns that will help after
		retirement.
Stock options	10	You want mainly growth
Commodities	10	opportunities, are in a
Under-$20 listed stocks	25	medium tax bracket, and do
Blue chip stocks	20	not need more current
(bought below 10 times earnings)		income now.
Money market fund	15	
Gold coins	20	

	PERCENTAGE OF TOTAL CAPITAL	SUITABLE IF
Commodities	10	You are a young person
Under-$20 listed stocks	35	who can pass up current
Blue chip stocks	15	income in favor of long-term
(bought below 10 times earnings)		growth.
Highly mortgaged real estate	20	
Gold coins	10	
Gold stocks	10	
Commodities	10	You are a well-to-do person
Penny stocks	5	in a high tax bracket.
Strategic metals	10	
Gold coins	25	
Tax-free bonds	30	
Treasury bills	10	
Farmland	10	
Stock options	10	You are an aggressive
Stocks of any type bought to *sell*	40	trader who wants a chance
options against		to expand capital with low
Money market fund	10	overall risk.
Silver coins	20	
Gold coins	20	
(And short-selling commodity futures against both gold and silver coins)		

A great many other variations are possible. Even if you are a person of modest means, you could go into more tactics than I have shown in any one of these samples—more combinations of small commitments in penny stocks, under-$20 stocks, blue chips, gold stocks, and utilities stocks. You could also consider the sale of options against stocks already held, and short-sale of futures against coins already held (see Chapter 19)—both of which require very little additional cash. But it is not the number of items that makes the main difference, it is the careful balancing of investments that complement each other.

For example, the heart of plan No. 2 is the equal commitment to a corporate bond fund and a money market fund. This technique, which was spelled out in the chapter on bonds, means that no change in the interest rate picture can damage your income. It might, however, damage your total worth because any sharpening of inflation would lessen the buying power of your dollars. That is why I cannot advise that some safety-minded investors split their entire capital between those two funds and forget anything else. They would very likely wind up with a steady amount of dollar income that would buy less and less. So in that plan, I have added some stocks, gold and silver coins to make up for the inflation loss.

Remember the Safety Net

In any personalized program that you make for yourself, be sure to embody the principle of balance and the provisions for protecting against inflation. Keep carefully in mind also the safety net that should be spread under each of these investments or speculations. Even in the highest-risk investments, there is always a way to prepare for and withstand the worst setbacks.

When you own stocks, whatever the price or quality, you should have stop-loss orders in place at times when you plan to be out of touch with your broker, so that any sudden adverse report that might blemish the company's outlook will not trap you in a long period of decline.

If you should go into stock options, there is a built-in precaution because the price of the option is all you can lose. Tell yourself in advance—and stick to it—that no amount of exciting new information will cause you to go beyond the amount of capital you have allocated to this purpose.

And when it comes to commodities, where there is literally no limit to how much you could lose if trapped into a reversing trend, you need to be firm about several disciplines: Never risk more than the predetermined percentage of your capital. Never be without a carefully set stop order that would get you out before any limit move could spring the trap. And never trade on the basis of hunches, feelings, emotions, or news stories.

Doing It Your Way

Finally, look back over the various tactics explained in this book, and think about *which ones appeal to you personally.* Not numbers or logic or risk-reward ratios, but which ones seem satisfying or enjoyable to go into. This is of great importance because we are all people before we are investors, or consumers, or anything else. If, as a person, you undertake things that are hard or distasteful to you, the chances of steady success are lessened. Even if you manage to push ahead through sheer determination, the reason for financial success is put into question.

So think about each subject and the variations that are possible in each one. Do you like the idea of reading stock market publications regularly, going over descriptions of various companies in your broker's research library, choosing and following a few stocks on your own? Or would you prefer to run down a list of mutual funds just once, select the one whose long-term performance seems best attuned to your needs, and then let that institution handle the stock portion of your capital?

Would you perhaps like to pass up the stocks altogether, but achieve some of the same results by the alternate route of using just a few per cent of your capital to buy highly volatile stock options and keeping the rest in income-producing assets?

Do you want to acquire a few gold coins, add to them at specified intervals, and simply hold them? Or is it appealing to think of also selling futures contracts against your holdings and trying for extra income?

Are you emotionally inclined toward the complex area of commodity trading or the much more sedate world of utilities stocks?

If the type of overall strategy that I have shown as being suitable to your financial condition also appeals to you from the standpoint of personal satisfaction, you are fortunate. For then you can quickly move ahead with a plan that is both pleasurable and likely to succeed.

Most people find that their inclination is to tie up their capital in assets that barely keep pace with inflation, because they are reluctant to attempt the more dynamic tactics that would get better results. If that proves to be true in your case, I urge you to look again at some of the techniques that have high ability to multiply capital.

You should not force yourself to go into anything that you cannot take interest in; but make an effort to understand it better before you decide. Techniques that first strike you as "too risky" often are just the opposite. For the deadliest peril in these times is to hold cash or static assets that give only the illusion of security. Unless a good part of your money is multiplying, you are sliding downhill.

There is a smaller number of persons who will find that their inclinations lead them to gamble too much—to stress dynamic investments without enough devoted to the patient ones that provide a balance. If your personal selections would give you a portfolio that is short on stability, you *must* turn some of your high-risk commitments into steady income producers.

The balanced portfolios shown above are designed to prepare you for both parts of the two-stage economic future that I have outlined for you. You will do best if you watch the various indicators outlined in this book and then adjust your holdings as the trend moves from Phase I to Phase II. But it is not a must. Selecting the new financial strategy that best suits your situation automatically puts you in a position that will adapt to the expected changes.

If you observe the rules I have mentioned for each investment technique and the suggested approach for the total package, you will gain. Some will profit more than others because of the obvious differences in resources, effort, and choice of plan. But the potential is there for *you* to be one of the winners.

Index

ADR's (American Depositary Receipts), 142
Airlines, 91
Alaska:
  petroleum in, 18
  resources of, 202
Alcoa, 44, 204
Aluminum, 200
American Home Products, 92
American Telephone & Telegraph, 92
Angell, George, 177
Angola, Zaire invaded by, 203
Antimony, 208
Antiques, 12, 22, 33–34, 50
Anyone Can Make A Million (Shulman), 168
Arab investors, 55–64, 149–150
Arbitrage, 196
Art collectibles, 12, 22, 30, 50
ASA Ltd., 140, 196
Assets:
  of Arabs, 60
  of companies, 92–93
  personal, 24, 132–133
Austerity, 4–5, 7, 17
Australia:
  diamonds in, 50
  mining stocks in, 203–204
Austria, gold coins minted by, 135
Automotive industry, 9, 18–19, 38
Autotrol, 20

Bache and Company, 206
Balance of payments, 185–186
Balance of trade, 185–186
Balance sheet, personal, 24–25
Bank of England, 120
Banks:
  foreign, 114
  gold mine stocks held by, 142
  Mexican, 109
  safe deposit boxes in, 137, 152
  savings accounts in, 109
  savings and loan, 105–106, 110–111
Barron's, 70
Bauxite, 202, 207
Bear market, 78, 94–95
Bergen Brunswig Corp., 79, 84
Bethlehem Steel, 68
"Big ticket" items, 9
Bimetallism, 147–148
Blue chip stocks, 27, 28, 43–45, 62, 93, 212–213
Blyvooruitzicht gold mine, 146
Bond funds, 99, 100, 102, 104–107, 212
Bond market, 97–107
  declines in, 15–16, 97
  as indicator, 69, 70–72, 83
  interest rates and, 83, 97–98, 101–102, 104, 114
Bonds, 27, 28, 29–30, 34–36, 45–46
  Arab investors in, 60
  "callable," 101

Bonds (*cont.*):
  discounted, 101–102
  high-yield, 103–104
  as investments, 46, 100
  "junk," 103
  long-term vs. intermediate, 100–101
  tax-free, 104–105, 213
  Treasury, 98, 101, 106
  utility, 101
Book value, 92–93
Booms, 183–184
Bracken gold mine, 146
Broken Hill Proprietary, 204
Bullion coins, 130
Bull market, 78

CAD/CAM (computer-aided design and computer-aided manufacturing), 18–19
Cadmium, 200
Canada:
  gold coins minted by, 132, 134–135
  gold mines in, 141
Capital:
  division of, 33–35
  safeguarding of, 39–40
Capital gains tax, 9
Capital Preservation Fund, 111
Cardinal Government Securities, 111
Carnation Company, 92
Cash:
  management of, 115–116
  stocks and, 81–82
Cash Reserve Management Fund, 112
Central America, petroleum in, 18–19
Certificates of deposit (CD's), 114
Chartists, 75
Chase Econometrics Associates, 66
Chicago, commodities market in, 167
China, People's Republic of, gold coins minted by, 131–132
Chromium, chromite, 202, 203, 207, 208
Chrysler Corporation, 44
Cincinnati-Milacron, 20
Clothing industry, 20–21
Coal, conversion to, 18
Cobalt, 200, 202, 203, 207, 208
Coins:
  Austrian, 135
  British, 135–136
  bullion, 130

  Canadian, 132, 134–135
  Chinese, 131–132
  dealers in, 136–137, 152, 195
  gold, 27, 28, 29, 36, 124, 125, 128–138, 139, 140, 212–213
  "junk," 152
  Mexican, 135
  rare, 131–132
  silver, 27, 28, 29, 36–37, 152, 154–155, 213
  South African, 133–134
  U.S., 37, 152
Coin World, 131
Collectibles, 12, 22, 30, 33–34, 37, 50–51
  art as, 12, 22, 30, 50
  coins as, 131–132
Colonial Sugar Refining Co., 204
Commodities, 27, 28, 29, 34, 40, 51, 166–179, 212–213, 214
  Arab investors in, 62–63
  averages in, 172–176
  currency as, 178, 180–188
  glossary of, 178–179
  gold as, 170, 196–199
  gold vs., 121–124
  guidebooks to, 177
  leverage in, 167–168, 181
  managed accounts in, 171–172
  silver as, 150, 153–155, 196–199
  traders in, 168–169, 182
  whipsaw problem in, 174–175
Companies:
  investing in, 87–96
  selection of, 92–95
Compounding, 105
Computer industry, 18–19, 21, 91
Computervision, 20
Con Edison, 44
Consumers, spending by, 9–10
Continental Corp., 92
Contracts, in commodities, 178
Copper, 200, 202
Coronas, 135
Crane, Burton, 43
Credit, 82
Cross & Trecker, 20
"Cross rates," 181–182
Currency:
  as commodity, 178, 180–188
  determinants of, 184–187

foreign, 11, 57, 109, 120, 122, 131–
132, 178, 180–188
paper, 11, 120–121, 124, 129, 148
precious metals vs., 119, 129
U.S., depreciation of, 10–12, 56, 57,
109, 129
(*See also* Coins)

Day Order, 178
Dean Witter Reynolds, 203
DeBeers cartel, 12, 49–50
"Defensive stop," 179
Deficits:
federal, 6–7, 8
of poor nations, 33
Deflation, 192
Depreciation, 9
Deutschemarks, 57, 182, 185, 187
Diamonds, 12, 22, 27, 28, 30, 49–50
gold vs., 120
Diversification, importance of, 31, 32–
40, 56, 164, 165
Dollars, Canadian, 180
Dollars, U.S.:
Arab holdings of, 56, 57
depreciation of, 10–12, 56, 57, 109,
129
speculation of, 180–181
Dome Mines, 141
Donoghue's Money Fund Report, 113
Doornfontein gold mine, 145
Dow Jones Industrial Average (DJIA),
44, 67, 68–72, 76, 89, 95
Drexel Burnham Lambert, Inc., 141,
203
Dreyfus bond fund, 102
Driefontein Consolidated, 142–143
DuPont, 68

Eastman Kodak Company, 45, 68, 149
Economic outlooks, 32–33
Economic Recovery Act (1981), 5–6, 8–
9
Economist (London), 187
Einstein, Albert, 105
Electromanganese, 208
Electronic revolution, 18–19, 21, 91
Electronics, consumer, 21
Energy:
conservation of, 32
price of, 18–19, 38

England:
Bank of, 120
currency of, 135–136, 185
gold coins minted by, 135–136
Engle, Louis, 72
Environmentalism, 202
Europe, trade with, 7–8, 11
European Common Market, 20
European Monetary System, 125
Evans, Michael, 66

Fannie Mae, 106
Farmers, as commodities sellers, 169
Farmland, as investment, 61–62, 213
Fastest Game in Town, The (Reinach),
177
Fast food industry, 91
Federal Credit Banks, 106
Federal deficits, 6–7, 8
Federal Home Loan Banks, 106
Federal Home Loan Mortgage Corp.,
106
Federal National Mortgage Association,
106
Federal Reserve Board, U.S., 4, 7, 82
Fidelity Funds, 102, 103
Financial goals, 23–31
Financial Times, 187
First Variable Rate Fund for Govern-
ment Income, 111
Fixed-rate pools, 114–115
Ford, Henry, 18
Ford Motors, 44
Foreign aid, 7–8
Francs, Swiss, 57, 180
Freddie Mac, 106
Free State Geduld, 144, 145
Fuel:
cost of, 18–19
(*See also* Energy; Oil)
Fundamental traders, 168–169, 182–
187
Futures (*see* Commodities)

Garment industry, 20–21
Gemstones, 12, 27, 28, 30
General Electric, 20, 44
General Motors, 38
Germanium, 200, 208
Germany:
currency of, 57, 180, 185, 187

Germany (*cont.*):
  inflation in, 122
  metals and minerals imported by,
    202
Glamor stocks, 26, 44
"Going long, going short," 178
Gold, 119–127
  Arab buyers of, 56, 57–58
  ban on ownership of, 128–129
  commodities vs., 121–124
  as commodity, 170, 196–199
  diamonds vs., 120
  inflation and, 11, 12, 107, 127, 128–
    129, 192
  interest rates and, 114
  investments based on, 125
  oil vs., 121, 151
  "paper," 124
  price increases in, 12–13, 22, 126–
    127
  price ratio of, 148, 194–196
  purchasing power of, 121–124
  selling of, 189–197
  silver vs., 120, 133, 147–148, 151,
    155, 194–196
Gold coins, 27, 28, 29, 36, 124, 125,
    128–138, 139, 140, 212–213
  bullion vs., 130
  insurance for, 137–138
  security for, 137–138
Gold mine stocks, 27, 28, 36, 38, 125,
    133, 139–146, 196, 212–213
  American, 141
  South African, 36, 38–39, 139–146
Goldplan AG, 193
Government Investors' Trust, 111
Grain complex, 178
Greenspan, Alan, 98
GTC (Good Till Cancelled), 178

Harmony, 38, 146
Hartebeestfontein, 38, 146
Hecla Mining, 196
Heim, Lawrence J., 40, 75–76
Hoffman, Kurt, 20
Holding companies, 140
Holiday Inns, 38
Homestake Mining Company, 141
Hong Kong, manufacturing in, 20
Hoover, Herbert, 6

Housing industry, 9, 38, 48, 170
Hunt brothers, 149–150

IBM, 20, 21, 30
Imports, policy on, 11
Indexes, of currencies, 182–183, 187–188
Indium, 200
Indonesia, petroleum in, 18–19
Industries:
  growing, 18–19, 90–92
  metals and minerals needed by, 200,
    202
Inflation, 3, 4, 10, 17, 32–33, 106, 108,
    183–185, 186
  in Germany, 122
  gold and, 11, 12, 107, 127, 128–129,
    192
  hedges against, 36–37, 107, 128, 192
  investments recommended during,
    27, 107
  money supply and, 82
  real estate and, 47–48
  in Spain, 148
"Inflation premium," 98, 106
Institutional Investor, 63–64
Interest rates:
  bond market and, 83, 97–98, 101–
    102, 104, 114
  gold and, 114
  government manipulation of, 183–184
  1981 policy on, 11
  "real," 185
  real estate and, 47
  recessions and, 183–184
  stock market and, 82, 114
  upward trend of, 4, 10, 32–35, 36, 83
Intergold Corp., 136
Intergraph, 20
International Monetary Fund, 124
Investment(s):
  analysis of, 25–31
  bonds as, 46, 100
  in companies, 87–96
  defined, 41
  flexibility of, 30–31
  gold-based, 125
  minimum, 112
  multiplying power of, 26–27
  for retirees, 29, 30, 34, 39, 100, 133,
    138, 147, 155, 210, 211, 212

speculation vs., 41–52, 77–78, 87, 100, 163, 204–205
stability of, 27–29
Investment Company Institute, 112
Investment Rarities, 136, 138
Iranian hostage crisis, 60

Japan:
currency of, 57, 185
microelectronics industry in, 19
trade with, 7–8, 11, 202
Jastram, Roy W., 121–122
Johannesburg Exchange, 142
Johns Manville, 38
Johnson & Johnson, 92
Journal of Commerce, 187
"Junk bonds," 103
"Junk coins," 152

Kansas City, commodities market in, 167
Kellogg, 92
Kemper Money Market Fund, 112
Kennecott, 44
Kloof Gold Mining Co., 143–144
Korean War, 203
Kroner, 135
Krugerrands, 133–134

Lead, 200, 202
Leslie gold mine, 146
Leverage:
in commodities, 167–168, 181
defined, 27, 167–168
of options, 159
in real estate, 47
Liabilities, personal, 24
Limit move, 179
Limit order, 179
"Liquidating," in commodities, 179
Liquidity, 29, 51, 58, 104
Lloyds of London, 206
LME (London Metals Exchange), 206
Loans:
Arab sources of, 59–60
"tied," 8
London:
commodities market in, 167
gold market in, 12, 142
Loraine gold mine, 146

Managed commodity accounts, 171–172
Manganese, 202, 207
Maple Leaf coins, 134
Margin, for silver futures, 154
Margin calls, 90
Marievale gold mine, 146
Market order, in commodities, 179
Marks, German, 57, 180, 185, 187
Maturity index, 113–114
Meat complex, 179
Merrill Lynch, 114–115
Merrill Lynch Corporate Bond Funds, 103
Merrill Lynch Government Securities Fund, 111
Metal detectors, 137, 152
Metals and minerals, 12–13, 28, 34, 114, 119, 200–208
(*See also specific metals*)
Mexico:
banks in, 109
currency of, 135, 180
gold coins minted by, 135
petroleum in, 18
Microelectronics, 18–19
Midwest, real estate values in, 48
Minicontracts, 178
Mining stocks:
Australian 203–204
gold, 27, 28, 36, 38, 125, 133, 139–146, 196
silver, 196
South African, 36, 38–39, 139–146
uranium, 38, 143, 145–146
"Mini-Rands," 134
Minneapolis, commodities market in, 167
MOC (Market On Close), 179
Money:
defined, 120
paper, 11, 120–121, 124, 129, 148
(*See also* Currency)
Money managers, 63–64, 69, 113, 172, 184
Money market funds, 34–35, 99, 104, 107, 108–116, 212–213
Money supply, 82–83
MOO (Market On Opening), 179
Morgan Guaranty Trust Company, 32

Mortgages, 47–48, 105
Moving averages, 172–176
Municipal bond funds, 104

National Academy of Sciences, 202
Net worth, personal, 24
News, stock market affected by, 81, 85
New York, commodities market in, 167
New York Times, 207
Nickel, 200
North Sea, petroleum in, 18–19
Nuclear power, 38
Numeraire, 121
Numismatics, 131

Oil:
    glut of, 18, 91
    gold vs., 121, 151
    prices of, 32–33, 38, 57
OPEC, 38
Oppenheimer Funds, 103
Options, 26, 27, 28, 34, 39, 51, 159–
        165, 196, 212–213, 214
    call vs. put, 161–162
    defined, 160
    leverage of, 159
    risks in, 159, 163–165
    silver, 153
Option spreads, 163
Organization for Economic Coopera-
        tion and Development, 19
Osmium, 13

Palladium, 13
Paper money, 11, 120–121, 124, 129,
        148
Patents, 18
Payments, balance of, 185–186
Penn Central, 44
P/E ratio, 93–94
Pesos, Mexican, 135, 180
Petroleum (*see* Oil)
Phelps Dodge, 44
"Pit," 167
Platinum, 13, 190, 202, 207
Politics, economics affected by, 3–13
Pounds, British, 120, 180, 185
Precious metals, 12–13, 28, 34, 114,
        119, 129
    (*See also specific metals*)

Precious Metals Holding Co., 140
President Brand Mines, 144
President's Council of Economic
        Advisers, 66
President Steyn Mines, 144
Productivity, 21, 185, 186

Reagan, Ronald, 5–6
Reagan Administration:
    goals of, 3–4
    incorrect judgments of, 4–5
    predictions about, 5–13, 17–18
Real estate, 22, 27, 28, 30, 33–34, 41–
        42, 46–49, 213
    Arab investors in, 56, 57, 58, 60–62
    inflation and, 47–48
    interest rates and, 47
    leverage in, 47
Recessions:
    interest rates and, 183–184
    prediction of, 66
Reinach, Anthony M., 169, 177
Republic National Bank, 136
Retail sales, 9
Retirement:
    investments and, 29, 30, 34, 39, 100,
        133, 138, 147, 155, 210, 211, 212
    precious metals for funding of, 189,
        192–193
Rhodium, 13, 200, 208
Risk, 42
    minimizing of, 101, 110–111, 163–
        165, 175, 188, 214
    of options, 159, 163–165
Rochester Telephone, 92
Roosevelt, Franklin D., 6, 8, 129
Rothschild, Nathan Meyer, Baron de,
        119
Rowe Price bond fund, 102
Rowe Price Prime Reserve Fund, 112
Rush, Howard, 20

Sadat, Anwar el-, 81
Safe deposit boxes, 137, 152
St. Helena gold mine, 144
Saudi Arabia, oil prices and, 19
Savings accounts, 109
Savings and loan industry, 105–106,
        110–111
Savings certificates, 34–35, 39–40, 99

Securities:
  fixed-income, 106
  high-yield, 103
Selenium, 200
Senate Subcommittee on Minerals,
    Materials and Fuels, U.S., 201
Shulman, Morton, 168
Sigma Government Securities, 111
Silver, 147–155
  as commodity, 150, 153–155, 196–
    199
  gold vs., 120, 133, 147–148, 151, 155,
    194–196
  options on, 153
  price increases in, 12–13, 149–150,
    151
  price ratio of, 148, 194–196
  production of, 149
  selling of, 189–197
Silver coins, 27, 28, 29, 36–37, 152,
    154–155, 212–213
Silver mine stocks, 196
Simple moving averages, 172–176
Sinclair, James, 207–208
Sophisticated Investor, The (Crane), 43
South Africa:
  gold coins minted by, 133–134
  gold-mines in, 36, 38–39, 139–146
South Korea, manufacturing in, 20
Sovereigns, English, 135–136
Soviet Union, metals and minerals ex-
    ported by, 201–202, 203
Soybean complex, 179
Spain, inflation in, 148
Special Drawing Rights (SDR), 124
Speculation:
  defined, 41
  investment vs., 41–52, 77–78, 87,
    100, 163, 204–205
Split opening (or close), 179
Spread, in commodities, 179
Standard & Poor's (directory), 88
Standard & Poor's 500-stock average,
    68
Stilfontein gold mine, 146
Stock market, 65–76, 107, 126
  analysts of, 75
  Arab investors in, 57, 58, 62
  as barometer, 66–67
  bearish, 78, 94–95

bullish, 78
chartists in, 75
competition with, 81–82
declines in, 15, 44, 57, 65, 72–73,
    75–76, 89–90, 159
indicators in, 67–72
interest rates and, 82, 114
movement of, 79–81
news and, 81, 85–86
technicians in, 75
upturns in, 8–9, 65, 73–74
Stock options (*see* Options)
Stocks, 27, 28, 29–30, 34, 214
  balancing of, 37–39
  blue chip, 27, 28, 43–45, 62, 93,
    212–213
  book value of, 92–93
  buying of, 78, 83, 86
  cash and, 81–82
  as company shares, 87–96
  fashions in, 44–45
  glamor, 26, 44
  investing vs. trading in, 43–45
  mining (*see* Mining stocks)
  price/earnings ratio of, 93–94
  prices of, 83, 92, 95
  selection of, 92–95
  selling of, 78–79, 83, 86, 90
  trading of, 43, 77–86
  utilities, 27, 28, 46, 212
  vital signs of, 83–84
Stop order, in commodities, 179
Strategic Metals and Critical materials,
    Inc., 206
Sun Belt, real estate values in, 48
Sunshine Mining, 196
Switzerland:
  currency of, 57, 180
  gold policy of, 193

Taiwan, manufacturing in, 20
Takeovers, 84
Tantalum, 202
Taxes, 30, 164
  capital gains, 9
  cuts in, 5–6
Tax-free bonds, 104–105, 213
Tax shelters, 47
Technical traders, 169, 182, 187–188

Technicians, stock market, 75
Technological revolution, 18–19, 21, 91
Texas Utilities, 92
Textile industry, 20–21, 170
Third World, foreign aid to, 8
"Tied" loans, 8
Tin, 200
Titanium, 208
TLC (Too Late to Cancel), 179
Toronto, commodities market in, 167
Tourist industry, 38
Trade, balance of, 185–186
Treasury, U.S., 125, 128–129
Treasury bills, 26, 27, 28, 29, 34–35, 58, 106, 114, 213
Treasury bonds, 98, 101, 106

Unemployment, 3, 7–8, 186
Union Cash Management, 112
Unit Investment Trust, 114–115
Uranium, 38, 143, 145–146
U.S.S.R., metals and minerals exported by, 201–202, 203
U.S. Steel, 68
Utilities investments, 27, 28, 46, 101, 212

Vaal Reefs Exploration and Mining Co., 143
Value Line Cash Fund, 112
Vanadium, 207

Vanguard Funds, 103–104
"Volatile," 94
Volcker, John, 4, 7
Voltaire, 120

Wall Street Journal, 73, 141–142, 145, 187, 207
War:
  causes of, 16
  preparedness for, 18, 91
  threats of, 85
Warehouses, as investments, 60–61
Wealth:
  creation of, 15–16
  preservation of, 119
Wearables, 20–21
Welkom Mines, 145
Western Mining Corporation, 204
Westinghouse, 44
Whipsaw problem, 174–175
Winning in the Commodities Market (Angell), 177
Winnipeg, commodities market in, 167
Witwatersrand Nigel gold mine, 146
Woodman, Charles E., 69
World Bank, 8

Yen, Japanese, 57, 185

Zaire, cobalt in, 203
Zinc, 202
Zurich market, 12

About the Author

Charles A. Cerami is the Foreign Affairs and Investment Editor of the Kiplinger Washington Publications. As such, he has traveled widely and been in touch with leading statesmen and bankers in most of the European capitals. He is an accomplished linguist, speaking several languages fluently, and has been decorated by both the Italian and Belgian governments. His articles have appeared in leading magazines in the United States and Europe, including *Atlantic Monthly, Playboy, Nation's Business, Woman's Day, Town & Country, McCall's, Swiss Review of World Affairs, Spectator* of London, and *Optima* of South Africa.